what's it mean to be a baptist?

a short explanation about "doing church" the baptist way

M. T. Robbins

Copyright © 2019 M. T. Robbins

All rights reserved.

ISBN:
ISBN-13: 9781797490069

Scripture quotations are from The ESV® Bible (The Holy Bible, English Standard Version®), copyright © 2001 by Crossway, a publishing ministry of Good News Publishers. Used by permission. All rights reserved.

DEDICATION

I dedicate this book to Baptist pastors and local churches across the world. May they balance zeal for Biblical polity with love and kindness to our brothers and sisters in Christ who disagree.

Contents

INTRODUCTION 1
   Why it all Matters 2
   B-A-P-T-I-S-T Spells Baptist ... or Does It? 3
1: ALL ABOUT THE CHURCH 7
   The Local Church 9
      How Do You Define the Local Church? 11
2: ONLY THE NEW TESTAMENT TELLS US HOW TO "DO CHURCH" 36
3: ONLY PROFESSING CHRISTIANS CAN BE CHURCH MEMBERS 38
   The New and Better Covenant 39
      Ezekiel 11:17-20 39
      Ezekiel 16:59-63 40
      Ezekiel 36:24-31 41
      Zechariah 9:11-12 42
      Hebrews 10:11-22 43
      Contrast Between Covenants 44
   The Great Divide 46
4: WHO CAN BE BAPTIZED? 51
   The Presuppositional Divide 53
   What Does Baptism Mean? 56
      Acts 2:37-41 56
      Acts 8:12-13 57
      Acts 8:34-38 58
      Acts 10:44-48 58

- Acts 16:14-15 59
- Acts 16:29-34 60
- Acts 18:8 61
- Acts 19:1-7 62
- Acts 22:16 63
- Romans 6:1-11 63
- 1 Corinthians 1:13-16 66
- 1 Corinthians 6:9-11 67
- 1 Corinthians 12:12-13 67
- Galatians 3:23-27 68
- Ephesians 4:1-6 69
- Colossians 2:8-15 69
- Titus 3:3-7 71
- Hebrews 10:19-22 72
- 1 Peter 3:19-22 72
- Summary of Baptism 73

5: HOW IS BAPTISM DONE? 75
- What the Word "Baptism" Means 77
  - 2 Kings 5:14 77
  - Judith 12:7 78
  - Isaiah 21:4 78
  - Matthew 3:16 79
  - Mark 7:3-4 80
  - John 3:23 81
  - Acts 8:36-39 81
  - 1 Corinthians 10:2 81

Conclusion about the Word "Baptism"	82
The Holy Spirit, Baptism and Washing Metaphors	82
6: BAPTISTS ON THE LORD'S SUPPER	**94**
Who is the Lord's Supper For?	96
The Gospels	96
1 Corinthians 11	99
Is Christ "in" the Lord's Supper?	99
The Roman Catholic View	100
The Lutheran View	101
The Reformed View	103
The Memorial View	104
Are Baptism and Church Membership Requirements to Observe the Lord's Supper?	105
Arguments for believer's baptism and church membership as prerequisites for the lord's supper	107
Summing Up	113
Suggestions for Local Churches	114
7: LOCAL CHURCHES GOVERN THEMSELVES	**117**
A Survey of Church Government from the Book of Acts	118
From Stephen's murder to Paul's first missionary journey	119
Acts 15 and the so-called "Jerusalem Council"	121
The Dogma of Acts 16:4	123
The second missionary journey	125
Third missionary journey	126
Summary of the evidence from the book of Acts	127
What Form of Church Government is Biblical?	128
What is "congregational government?"	130

8: THE ONLY CHURCH OFFICERS ARE PASTORS AND DEACONS 135

The Office of an Apostle 136

The Office of the Pastor 139

The title of the "pastor" 139

The job of the pastor 140

Qualifications of a pastor 145

Number of pastors 147

The Office of the Deacon 149

Other Forms of Church Government 151

Episcopal government 151

Presbyterian government 153

Congregational government 155

9: EACH CHRISTIAN IS A PRIEST FOR GOD 157

10: EVERY PERSON HAS FREEDOM OF CONSCIENCE 165

Baptist Beginnings 167

What's the Point? 174

11: CONCLUSION – why you should care, and how churches can begin fixing things 177

What Should We Do? 178

Pastors should regularly teach and preach the distinction between the Old and New Covenants. 179

Pastors should teach periodic courses on comparative denominations, and focus particular attention on church membership, infant baptism, and the membership of the New Covenant. 179

Pastors should make a dedicated, concerted effort to make believer's baptism meaningful in the life of the church. 180

Pastors should make a dedicated effort to make the Lord's Supper

- a meaningful event for growth and sanctification in the local church. 182
- Pastors' should make a deliberate effort to ensure "new believers" are *actually believers*, before allowing them to officially join the congregation. This will make membership actually mean something. 183
- Pastors should commit to practicing redemptive church discipline. 184

What's in a Name? 187

APPENDIX 1 - THE CHRISTIAN AND GOVERNMENT 188

How Do We Do This in "Real Life?" 204

- The christian cake baker 205
- Was the American Revolution unbiblical? 207
- Pre-Civil War era fugitive slave laws 208
- Oregon's recent abortion law 211

Back to the Present Day 212

- Respect all men 215
- Love the family of believers 216
- Always have fearful reverence for God 216
- Always respect the Emperor 216

BIBLIOGRAPHY 217

Scripture Index 227

Acknowledgments

I'm grateful to the faculty of Maranatha Baptist Seminary (Watertown, WI) for teaching me to know, love and study the Scriptures. Hopefully, they'll still be willing to claim me as a graduate after reading this volume!

INTRODUCTION

Too many Christians don't know what it means to "be a Baptist." Even members of Baptist churches sometimes don't understand what makes them "different" than the Presbyterians across the street. This is too bad, because all this really does matter. There are two bad reactions to this situation, and you may have encountered one or both of them:

1. You pretend none of the differences matter, because all true Christians are united with Christ – no matter what the name on the building says!

This is the approach many Christians take today, in the contemporary West. After all, isn't the Gospel more important than disagreements over "how to do church?" Shouldn't we focus our energies on teaching about the Trinity, God, Christ and the doctrine of salvation? Does "being Baptist" really rank up there with these topics?

The problem is that once a person comes to faith, he has to be integrated into a local community of believers. What does that community look like? What is it *supposed* to look like? How should it be structured? How does it run? Who's in charge? What defines a "church," anyway?

So, you see, it *does* matter. But, it's dangerous to lurch to the opposite extreme …

2. You make the differences matter so much, that you despise all churches that aren't just like yours.

This is the other side of the coin. Some Baptists think the doctrine of the church is so important that all other churches really don't qualify as "churches" at all. The logic goes something like this; (a) if the Bible teaches a Baptist way of "doing church," then (b) any organization that doesn't follow this model is disobedient, and (c) isn't really a "church" at all!

To be sure, there are different degrees and flavors of this position. Some would boldly say Presbyterians, for example, don't have legitimate "churches" at all. They'd never recommend a new believer go there, and would be very doubtful they were even Christians. Others would be more cautious and tap-dance freely on the subject, but still follow that general pattern.

Why it all Matters

I believe "being Baptist" matters, because it's the way God wants His New Covenant community to function. But, I don't think "Baptist" is an umbrella term for theological orthodoxy. There are plenty of Methodists, Presbyterians and Nazarenes (etc.) who are Christians. I just think their way of "doing church" is terribly wrong, and I hope they see the error of their ways. This might seem like silly, ivory tower nit-picking. After all, who cares as long as you love Jesus, right?

Wrong.

Imagine that a group of eager, young Christians gather at a local Starbucks every Sunday for a bible study at 11:00 a.m. A different "leader" takes a turn every week reading a passage of Scripture and explaining it. The group always has a wonderful discussion. "The Spirit is, like, *really moving* in our lives," one attender explains, eyes alight with joy.

Once per month or so ("whenever we feel the Spirit leading us"), they observe the Lord's Supper together. But, they like being ... *different*. So, the group usually observes the ordinance with Cheese-Its and Diet Coke. They tried pita crackers and almond milk once. It didn't go over so well. It was . . . gross.

One attender explains he doesn't feel the need to go to a "traditional church."

> It's, like, so confining. I used to go to a 'normal' church, but it just became, like, way too much. All the rules. All the stuff that just, you know, like, gets in the way. I like coming here better. It's like we're getting back to the, you know, the . . . the purity that Jesus always talked about. Here, we just keep it simple. No rules. No judgment. Just the Word and the Spirit. I've grown in Christ more here than I ever did in a traditional church. When the Spirit is working, who am I to judge or criticize, ya know?

Does this young man go to a "church"? Is his Starbucks fellowship a church? Why, or why not? You see? It does matters what a "church" really is, and what it isn't. More specifically, for my purposes in this little book, it matters how you structure and organize the church. It matters how you "do church." And for that, we must turn to the New Testament.

B-A-P-T-I-S-T Spells Baptist ... or Does It?

Many Baptists have suffered through tedious sermon series on the "Baptist distinctives." You know the ones. The pastor typically flashes the acrostic "B - A - P - T - I - S – T" on a screen:

- **B**ible alone
- **A**utonomy of the local church

- **P**riesthood of the believer
- **T**wo ordinances; believer's baptism and the Lord's Supper
- **I**ndividual soul liberty
- **S**eparation of church and state
- **T**wo offices; pastor and deacon

... and then sallies forth to explain these doctrines.[1] The full story is a bit more complicated. Being "Baptist" is not simply about "baptism by immersion," and we aren't called this "because John the Baptist was the first Baptist."

And, interestingly, Baptists aren't a strict confessional denomination in the same way (for example) the Presbyterians or the Lutherans are. There is a remarkable diversity of thought in Baptist life over the specific "behind the scenes" details of how God saves sinners (e.g. election), the role of the Spirit (e.g. effectual calling, are sign gifts for today?, etc.), the role of the New Covenant for Christian life today, the details about the last days, interpretive frameworks (e.g. dispensational, covenental, etc.) and more.

This can't be emphasized enough; Baptists are not a "denomination" in the traditional sense. As one author put it:

> *Baptists, let it be repeated, are not in essence a "denomination" at all. Their stripes or spots may be deep-dyed but are not all found uniformly and consistently in all those families of Christians called by that name. Casual observers, and editors of major encyclopedias, conclude that it is the 'Baptist mode of baptism,' i.e. immersion, that marks of the*

---

1. According to historian David Beale (*Baptist History in England and America: Personalities, Positions, and Practices* [Maitland: Xulon Press, 2018; Kindle ed.], KL 127-134), the B-A-P-T-I-S-T acrostic was developed by L. Duane Brown in his 1969 book *Biblical Basis for Baptists* (1969). In 2009, Brown and his son released an updated edition.

Baptist species. The shallowness of this judgment is exposed easily.[2]

Instead, Baptists coalesce around several mutually-supporting doctrines **about the church.** Many of these distinctives aren't "Baptist," strictly speaking. For example, you can find them emphasized by other denominations. But, when you consider all these doctrines together as a unit, you have a Baptist congregation. You and your neighbor may each have milk, eggs, flour, vanilla and other ingredients in your kitchens. But, *only you* know how to combine them together to create that special, tasty dessert; the secret recipe your mother handed down to you and swore you to secrecy about so long ago …

So it is with these "Baptist distinctives." When you combine each "Baptist distinctive" together into a baking pan, in a very specific way according to that secret recipe, and put them into the oven @ 350 for 20 minutes, a Baptist will pop out of the oven.

In this book, I'll provide a discussion of these distinctives and some of the important theological implications. This won't be a dry recitation of the "B - A - P - T - I - S – T" acrostic, though. There are eight mutually supporting characteristics which generally distinguish Baptists from other churches:

1. Only the New Testament tells us how to "do church"
2. Only professing Christians can be church members
3. Baptism is an ordinance for believers that symbolizes and pictures a new believer's identification and union with Christ's death and resurrection, as well as a washing and cleansing from sins and the sinner's adoption into God's new covenant family

---

2. Jack Hoad, *The Baptist: An Historical and Theological Study of the Baptist Identity* (London: Grace, 1986), 10.

4. The Lord's Supper is only for Christians, and it's a vehicle God gave His people to memorialize and remember Christ's broken body, shed blood, and His imminent return
5. Local churches govern themselves
6. The only church officers are pastors and deacons, and there is no bureaucratic hierarchy or office in the Christian faith higher than these offices
7. Every Christian is a priest for God
8. Every Christian has freedom of conscience

Some readers may notice this is a "big-tent" definition of Baptist identity. I've deliberately not mentioned some distinctive "add-ons" from the Baptist fundamentalist movement (my own movement) which I think are important, but irrelevant to "being a Baptist."

The overriding mark of the Baptist identity is a single-minded desire to "do church" the way the Bible says. As one theologian remarked, "Other denominations will affirm their belief in the absolute authority of Scripture. No denominations have tried to consistently apply the absolute authority of Scripture to the doctrine of the Church like the Baptists."[3]

---

3. Larry Oats, "GPA 614 - Baptist Policy," Summer 2013, unpublished class notes (Watertown: Maranatha Baptist Seminary).

1: ALL ABOUT THE CHURCH

SYNOPSIS:

1. There is a corporate church, which is made up of all God's New Covenant people. There is also a local church, made up of New Covenant members in specific congregations all over the world.
2. The description and purpose of a local church that it is:
    a. a formal group of believers,
    b. in covenant with God and each other,
    c. who have been baptized by immersion after a profession of faith,
    d. who preach the Gospel individually and as a congregation with the goal of making Christian disciples,
    e. who practice the ordinances of believer's baptism and the Lord's Supper,
    f. who gather together weekly both to learn about God and all that He has commanded His people from the Bible,
    g. and for fellowship, encouragement, prayer and worship of God.
3. The classic "marks" or characteristics of a local church are unity, holiness, catholicity and apostolicity
4. Some more helpful marks of a local church are:
    a. it's in covenant with God and each other
    b. it glorifies God
    c. it dependent on the Holy Spirit
    d. it's focused on spiritual growth, not necessarily numerical growth
    e. it's fixated on Christ and the gospel
    f. it's absolutely committed to the Scriptures
    g. it's looking for Christ's return

The church is a New Covenant organization, and it didn't exist until the New Covenant was inaugurated with Jesus' perfect life, sacrificial and substitutionary death, and His miraculous resurrection. I'll explain more about this New Covenant distinction in a later chapter. But, it's enough to know now that the term "church" can mean two things in Scripture. To make things simple, I'll call them "big church" and the "local church."[4]

1. "Big church" means anyone who has become a believer from the time of Pentecost onward, and been made a member of the New Covenant.[5]
2. "Local church" means an individual, local congregation somewhere in the world.

It's a fact that the "big church" won't ever meet together in one place until Christ returns and gathers all believers to Himself.[6] As the Apostle Paul wrote:

---

4. Edward Hiscox states the matter plainly and simply: "In the 'Christian sense' the word *Ekklesia* has a two-fold signification in the New Testament. *First,* it is used, in its primary and literal sense, to designate a visible, local congregation of Christian disciples, meeting for worship, instruction and service. *Second,* it is used in a secondary and figurative sense, to designate the invisible, universal company, including all of God's true people on earth and in heaven.

   There is, then, the visible, local church, and the invisible, universal Church. In the latter case the word represents a conception of the mind, having no real existence in time or place, and not a historical fact, being only an ideal multitude without organization, without action, and without corporate being," (*Principles and Practices for Baptist Churches* [Philadelphia: Judson Press, 1894; reprint, Grand Rapids: Kregel, n.d.], 23-24).

5. I take the view that the church is a New Covenant body, distinct from the nation of Israel in the Old Covenant. I won't defend that view here, but the reader should be aware I hold to it. Some dispensationalists would disagree. They're in the minority.

6. Richard Clearwaters wrote: "Many individuals who will be members of the universal church body have never been born; other members of the universal church body are now asleep in Jesus while their bodies have never been resurrected or glorified. The universal church, therefore, has never been assembled or had a meeting. It is a prospective Church . . . If part of the membership is now in heaven, another part on earth, another part not yet born, there is as yet no assembly except in prospect," (*The Local Church of the New Testament* [Minneapolis: Central Press, 1959], 9-10).

> *For the Lord himself will descend from heaven with a cry of command, with the archangel's call, and with the sound of the trumpet of God. And the dead in Christ will rise first; then we who are alive, who are left, shall be caught up together with them in the clouds to meet the Lord in the air; and so we shall always be with the Lord (1 Thess 4:16-17).*

Because the "big church" has never been in one place at one time, it isn't always practical to talk about "the church" in this way. That's why when Christ or the Apostles talk about "the church," they often mean a *local group* of believers. That's the focus of this book. Here's a working definition of "the church" that encompasses both elements:

> *Scripture teaches there is both (1) a universal, dispersed, corporate body of Christ, made up of all New Covenant believers since Pentecost, which is organized and structured into (2) independent, local congregations of Christian disciples — the local church.*[7]

The Local Church

Since the church began at Pentecost, folks who have tried to be obedient to Scripture have gathered together and organized themselves into local congregations, in whatever city, town or village they live in. Almost everything written to churches in the New Testament is to one or more local congregations, in *one* place, about

---

7. "The church is the people of God who have been saved through repentance and faith in Jesus Christ and have been incorporated into his body through baptism with the Holy Spirit. It consists of two interrelated elements: the universal church is the fellowship of all Christians that extends from the day of Pentecost until the second coming, incorporating both the deceased believers who are presently in heaven and the living believers from all over the world. This universal church becomes manifested in local churches," (Gregg R. Allison, *Sojourners and Strangers: The Doctrine of the Church,* Foundations of Evangelical Theology Series, ed. John S. Feinberg [Wheaton: Crossway, 2012], Kindle Locations 607-611).

how *that church* is supposed to run and operate.[8] Christians can (and have) extrapolated out from there and applied these principles to their own churches, but that's the point - these letters were written to individual local churches:

> *To the church of God which is **at Corinth** (1 Cor 1:2; 2 Cor 1:1).*

> *To the churches **of Galatia** (Gal 1:2).*

> *To all the saints in Christ Jesus who are **at Philippi**, with the bishops and deacons (Phil 1:1).*

> *To the saints and faithful brethren in Christ **at Colossae** (Col 1:2).*

> *To the church of **the Thessalonians** (1 Thess 1:1; 2 Thess 1:1).*

> *To the exiles of the Dispersion **in Pontus, Galatia, Cappadocia, Asia, and Bithynia** ... (1 Pet 1:1).*

> *To the twelve tribes in the Dispersion (James 1:1).*

Also, we shouldn't forget Christ spoke to seven individual churches in the Book of Revelation (Rev 1-3). So, even though there certainly is one "big church," composed of all New Covenant believers since Pentecost, it's a little too vague to talk about the "Christian Church" in that way. The "big church" is like local branches of a massive corporation. You may love Walmart, and be able to give reasons why. But, you've never visited *every* Walmart, have you?

---

8. Other letters are circular letters (e.g. Ephesians (maybe!), James, 1 Peter, 2 Peter, etc.). These were written to many individual churches, and meant to be passed on after reading. Still others were written to individuals (e.g. Philemon, 1 and 2 Timothy, Titus; 2 and 3 John).

What you really mean is that you love the Walmart's you've visited (and, sometimes, not even all of them!).

So, when you say, "I'm going to church," you really mean you're going to get together with a congregation of other Christians in your local area (wherever you are) to worship God. And, the Lord has structured Christians into local churches all throughout the world.

How Do You Define the Local Church?

It's important to realize a church is not a building and it's also not a denomination. But, how should we describe a church? By what it does, by its purpose, or by its characteristics?[9] Christians have used each of these methods over the years. I'll combine these elements (the local church's description, purpose, and characteristics) as I offer up my own approach, below.

Description and Purpose

We don't need to think very hard about what a church is supposed to be doing. Jesus told the apostles what He wanted them to do, and the Book of Acts is an inspired record of them carrying out that mission. If you're a Christian, then you're an important part of that mission, too. Jesus said,

> *Go therefore and make disciples of all nations, baptizing them in the name of the Father and of the Son and of the Holy Spirit, teaching them to observe all that I have commanded you ... (Mt 28:19-20).*

This statement is a summary of a local church's mission. I'll use this statement, along with the rest of the biblical data discussed

---

9. See Allison (*Sojourners and Strangers*, KL 991-1074).

elsewhere in this book, to explain a local church's description and purpose:

> *The local church is a formal group of believers in covenant with God and each other, who have been baptized by immersion after a profession of faith, who preach the Gospel individually and as a congregation with the goal of making Christian disciples, who practice the ordinances of believer's baptism and the Lord's Supper, and who gather together weekly both to learn about God and all that He has commanded His people from the Bible, and for fellowship, encouragement, prayer and worship of God.*

Here are the building blocks of this definition:

1. **A formal group of believers in covenant with God and each other**

Baptists believe a church is a New Covenant community, and the New Covenant is only made up of believers who've repented of their sins and believed in who Jesus Christ is (the eternal Son of God), and what He's done (a sinless life in our place, a substitutionary, sacrificial death for our sins, and a miraculous resurrection to defeat Satan, sin and death).

And, this community is *formal*. This means there is membership and mutual accountability. It isn't a social club you float in or out of at will. It's formal membership in one of God's local embassies for His coming Kingdom.[10] The church is an advance base for God's future Kingdom, and its members are each consular officers.

---

10. "Most embassies represent a kingdom across geographic space. The local church is an embassy representing Christ's rule across eschatological time," (Jonathan Leeman, "A Congregational Approach to Unity, Holiness and Apostolicity: Faith and Order," in *Baptist Foundations: Church Government for an Anti-Institutional Age* [Nashville: B&H, 2015; Kindle ed.], KL 6340-6341).

2. **who have been baptized by immersion after a profession of faith,**

Baptists believe that baptism is for believer's only (i.e. "believer's baptism"), and the way this ordinance is described in the New Testament means baptism ought to be done by immersion in water (see ch. 4 for more on this).

3. **who preach the Gospel individually and as a congregation with the goal of making Christian disciples**

This is the first of the two main pillars of a church's mission. A congregation preaches the Gospel with the goal of making disciples. To be sure, a Christian can't control whether a person accepts or rejects the Gospel. All thinking Christians should agree with one Baptist confession when it says, "regeneration consists in giving a holy disposition to the mind; that it is effected in a manner above our comprehension by the power of the Holy Spirit, in connection with divine truth, so as to secure our voluntary obedience to the gospel …"[11]

But, the point is that a church must be about preaching the Gospel. This isn't just a corporate activity the church does on Saturday mornings, for example. It's an individual activity each member does, day in and day out, in whatever small orbit and sphere of influence God has given him. A Christian's self-identity, and his church's self-identity, must be wrapped up in this all-consuming mission. We must have the same mindset the Apostle Peter had, when he reminded the Christians in Asia Minor that,

---

11. 1833 *New Hampshire Confession of Faith* (Article 7); from William L. Lumpkin, *Baptist Confessions of Faith,* revised ed. (Valley Forge: Judson, 1969), 363 – 364.

you believers are a chosen people, a royal priesthood, a holy nation – God's own people. The purpose of all this is so you'd announce the wonderful things God did, who called you out of the darkness [and] into His amazing light. You used to not be a people, but now you're the people of God! You weren't given any mercy, but now you've received mercy (1 Pet 2:9-10).[12]

4. who practice the ordinances of believer's baptism and the Lord's Supper,

Believer's baptism is the act that formally initiates a Christian into God's family. It doesn't "do anything" in and of itself, but it publicly affirms what Father, Son and Spirit have done in a sinner's life. The Lord's Supper is a time of renewal, where Christians gather to remember Christ's broken body and shed blood, all done for sinners, and to look forward to the time when He'll return for His adopted children. It's also a time for self-examination and serious introspection.

5. and who gather together weekly both to learn about God and all that He has commanded His people from the Bible

This is the second pillar of a local church's mission; the first is to preach the Gospel. A congregation gathers once per week (or more) to learn about God. This is best done through the steady, systematic, expository preaching of God's word. Jesus said the apostles had to *first* make disciples, *then* teach them to do what He commanded. Father, Son and Spirit are the authors of Scripture, so *all* of God's word tells the Christian what he needs to know.

The Apostle Peter tells us "his divine power has granted to us all things that pertain to life and godliness, through the knowledge of him

---

12. This is my own translation.

who called us to his own glory and excellence," (2 Pet 1:3), and God has preserved that "knowledge of Him" in the inspired Scriptures. The Spirit never works at cross-purposes from the Bible, and Jesus said the Spirit "will teach you all things, and bring to your remembrance all that I have said to you," (Jn 14:26).

Christians learn what God has commanded them by studying His word, both individually and as a congregation.

6. **and for fellowship, encouragement, prayer and worship of God.**

When a congregation gathers, its purpose is not to draw unbelievers into the services. To be sure, that would be lovely! But, the primary purpose is for God's New Covenant people to work together for the cause of the Gospel, encourage one another, pray together and, above all, worship our triune God above.

Classic Marks of a Church

So far, so good; but what does a local church look like? What does it do, and how does it do it? There are four classic "marks" of a church that many theologians and church traditions discuss. Depending on who you're talking to and where he's coming from, these can mean different things. These marks are:[13]

1. **Unity**

This means all true Christians are united under Christ. As the Apostle Paul wrote, "there is one body and one Spirit, just as you were called to the one hope that belongs to your call, one Lord, one faith, one baptism, one God and Father of us all, who is above all and

---

13. See especially Hiscox (*Principles and Practices,* 31 - 35).

through all and in all," (Eph 4:4-6). This is a *spiritual* unity, not an outward, visible one. That is, every true Christian can fellowship with another (whatever else their inter-family differences are) on the basis of shared salvation in Jesus Christ.[14]

2. Holiness

Christians have been declared holy and righteous by God because they have believed in who Christ is and what He's done. God did this "by imputing Christ's active obedience unto the whole law, and passive obedience in his death for their whole and sole righteousness by faith, which faith they have not of themselves; it is the gift of God."[15] Of course, Christians never act holy all the time. But, we've been *declared to be* holy because we've been given Christ's righteousness, and our job is to systematically put to death old sins and replace them with holy thoughts and actions bit by bit, millimeter by millimeter, day by day.

True Christians will *want* to do this, even though they won't always succeed. To the extent individual Christians are holy, congregations are holy, too. This is always a work in progress.[16]

---

14. As Michael Bird, an Anglian theologian from Australia, observed, "The oneness of the church, then, is christological, with Christ as the head of one body; it is Trinitarian with church unity emulating the unity of Father, Son, and Spirit; it is kerygmatic as it is rooted in one evangelical faith; it is sacramental as it shares one baptism and partakes of one loaf; and it is visible since unity is expressed in tangible relationships with others," (Michael F. Bird, *Evangelical Theology: A Biblical and Systematic Introduction* [Grand Rapids: Zondervan, 2013; Kindle ed.], KL 16703-16706).

15. 1689 *London Baptist Confession of Faith* (11.1). Obtained on 15 November 2018 from the Center for Reformed Theology and Apologetics, at https://reformed.org/documents/index.html.

16. The Belgic Confession (1619) has some wise comments on this: "With respect to those who are members of the Church, they may be known by the marks of Christians, namely, by faith; and when they have received Jesus Christ the only Saviour, they avoid sin, follow after righteousness, love the true God and their neighbor, neither turn aside to the right or left, and crucify the flesh with the works thereof. But this is not to be understood as if there did not remain in them great infirmities; but they

3. **Catholicity**

This means local churches understand and recognize that God is at work in all true churches, throughout all the world, no matter what flavor of Christianity they belong to. It's closely related to the mark of unity (above). "Catholicity is recognizing that God is at work in other places and in other churches, drawing men and women to himself and drawing them together under the banner of Jesus Christ."[17]

Of course, a church is not really "Christian" at all if it denies the components of the Gospel, who Jesus is, who God is, and what the Gospel accomplishes for all who repent and believe.[18] But, the fact is that Baptists don't have a corner on the Christian market.

4. **Apostolicity**

This isn't about tracing a line of visible succession back to the time of the apostles, as the Roman Catholic Church and the Landmark Baptists[19] would have us do. It's about tracing a *perpetuity of apostolic Christian doctrine*.[20] If a church teaches the true "rule of faith" that

---

> fight against them through the Spirit all the days of their life, continually taking their refuge in the blood, death, passion, and obedience of our Lord Jesus Christ, in whom they have remission of sins through faith in him," (Philip Schaff, "The Belgic Confession," Article 29, in *The Creeds of Christendom*, 3 vols. [New York: Harper & Brothers, 1882], 3:420.

17. Bird *(Evangelical Theology,* KL 16752 – 16754).

18. This last bit, about what the Gospel accomplishes, is why the Roman Catholic Church cannot be considered a Christian church.

19. On Landmark Baptist polity, see especially H. Leon McBeth, *The Baptist Heritage: Four Centuries of Baptist Witness* (Nashville: B&H, 1987), 447 – 461. See also David Beale, *Historical Theology In-Depth: Themes and Contexts of Doctrinal Development Since the First Century,* 2 vols. (Greenville: BJU Press, 2013), 2:186 – 193. See also Tyler Robbins, "What is 'Landmarkism?' A Quick Look at a Strange Baptist Polity," *Eccentric Fundamentalist,* published on August 6, 2014 at https://bit.ly/2IAn5rA.

Christians have always believed and preached, straight from the Bible, then it's an "apostolic" congregation.

More Specific Characteristics of a Church

The classic characteristics are good, but they're rather vague and abstract; they don't leave you with much to hold on to.[20] Here, I've formulated a more specific list of "marks" that will help us get a better handle on the characteristics of a healthy local church:[21]

Marks of a Healthy Local Church	
1	*In covenant with God and each other*
2	*Glorifies God*
3	*Dependent on the Holy Spirit*
4	*Spiritual growth*
5	*Fixated on Christ and the gospel*
6	*Absolutely committed to the Scriptures*
7	*Looking for Christ's return*

These characteristics define what a church is and what it should do. If an organization doesn't do these things, then it can be called many things, but it isn't a church in the New Testament sense at all. Here, I'll briefly explain what these characteristics mean.

1. **A local church is full of people who are in covenant with God and each other**

Church members are in covenant with God because He's saved them, and made them members of the New and better covenant through His eternal Son, Jesus Christ. Being a Christian means a radical

---

20. Hiscox (*Principles and Practices,* 33).

21. See especially John S. Hammett, *Biblical Foundations for Baptist Churches: A Contemporary Ecclesiology* (Grand Rapids: Kregel, 2005), 61 - 62.

shift in priorities and self-identity (see 1 Pet 2:4-10, and the entire book of 1 Peter). It means you want to live for the Lord, and not for yourself. Again, the Apostle Peter has some good insight for us:

> *So, because Christ suffered in the body, you also must arm yourselves [with] the same mindset, because the one who is suffering in the body is now through with sin, to no longer live the rest of his life according to men's lusts, but instead according to God's will. Because enough time has now passed [for you] to have accomplished the desire of unbelievers. You used to live a life of debauchery, wicked lusts, drunkenness, wild celebrations, drinking parties and disgusting idol worship (1 Pet 4:1-3).[22]*

God saves Christians to make them His priests, so they'd represent Him and mediate the Gospel to the world. "We are his workmanship, created in Christ Jesus for good works, which God prepared beforehand, that we should walk in them," (Eph 2:10). Our job is to serve Him because we're His covenant children. And, our job is to also serve one another:

> *Now, the end of everything has now drawn near, so be sensible and self-controlled for the sake of [your] prayers. Above all else, always keep [your] love for one another constant, because love always covers many sins.*
>
> *Be hospitable to one another without complaining. To the degree that each [of you] has received a gift, use it to serve one another, like good servants of God's multifaceted grace. If someone speaks, [do it like he's speaking] God's [very] words. If someone serves, [he must do so] from the strength that God*

---

22. This is my own translation.

always supplies, so that God will be glorified in all things through Jesus Christ.

To him [belongs] the glory and sovereignty for ever and ever! Amen (1 Pet 4:7-11).[23]

When I say church members are in covenant *with each other,* I mean they understand they have obligations to one another. It'd be nice if we could take that for granted, but we can't. The fact is that many Baptist churches (indeed, many churches in general) don't take church membership seriously, so the members don't take it seriously, either. I knew one senior enlisted man in the Navy who had this motto in his email signature block, "acceptable behavior becomes an acceptable standard." I've never forgotten that, because it's true. If churches don't take membership seriously, then the people won't either. This is where the idea of a formal church covenant comes into the picture.

A church covenant is an attempt to make what Peter wrote (1 Pet 4:7-11) a reality in the life of a congregation. It explains to new members what's expected of them. They're expected to serve. They're expected to pray for one another. They're expected to pray for the pastors. They're expected to *be there* for one another. They're expected to hold one another accountable. In short, they're supposed to love one another. As one Baptist theologian explained, a church covenant makes it "clear that church membership involved a commitment that any regenerate person should accept."[24]

Here's an example of perhaps the most famous Baptist church covenant, written by J. Newton Brown in 1853. This gives you an idea

---

23. This is my own translation.

24. Hammett (*Biblical Foundations,* 117). See especially Hammett's outstanding discussion about how to reorganize an existing church around a new church covenant in order to make membership meaningful again (116 – 120).

of what a church covenant looks like, and allows you to "see" what the concept is:[25]

> **Church Covenant by J. Newton Brown (1853)**
>
> Having been led, as we believe, by the Spirit of God to receive the Lord Jesus Christ as our Saviour; and, on the profession of our faith, having been baptized in the name of the Father, and of the Son, and of the Holy Ghost, we do now, in the presence of God, angels, and this assembly, most solemnly and joyfully enter into covenant with one another, as one body in Christ.
>
> We engage, therefore, by the aid of the Holy Spirit, to walk together in Christian love; to strive for the advancement of this church, in knowledge, holiness, and comfort; to promote its prosperity and spirituality; to sustain its worship, ordinances, discipline, and doctrines; to contribute cheerfully and regularly to the support of the ministry, the expenses of the church, the relief of the poor, and the spread of the gospel through all nations.
>
> We also engage to maintain family and secret devotion; to religiously educate our children; to seek the salvation of our kindred and acquaintances; to walk circumspectly in the world; to be just in our dealings, faithful in our engagements, and exemplary in our deportment; to avoid all tattling, backbiting, and excessive anger; to abstain from the sale and use of intoxicating drinks as a beverage,[26] and to be zealous in our efforts to advance the kingdom of our Saviour.
>
> We further engage to watch over one another in brotherly love; to remember each other in prayer; to aid each other in sickness and distress; to cultivate Christian sympathy in feeling and courtesy in speech; to be slow to take offense, but always ready for reconciliation, and mindful of the rules of our Saviour, to secure it without delay.

---

25. Brown's covenant can be found in many locations online, and in many printed publications, too. See especially the *Baptist Center for Theology and Ministry*, operated by the New Orleans Baptist Theological Seminary, at http://www.baptistcenter.net/confessions page.html.

26. Because of the comment where church members promise "to abstain from the sale and use of intoxicating drinks as a beverage," it's clear this covenant was the product of an American minister, and was written during the temperance movement in the United States.

> We moreover engage, that when we remove from this place, we will as soon as possible unite with some other church, where we can carry out the spirit of this covenant, and the principles of God's Word.

Here is another church covenant, which dates to 1798.[27] It was written by Samuel Jones, who authored the very first Baptist church manual in America. It's shorter and less well-known than Brown's covenant (above), but it's worth considering. Again, the point is the concept of church members being in covenant with each other:

> **Samuel Jones' Church Covenant (1798)**
>
> We, whose names are under written, being desirous to be constituted a church of Jesus Christ, in this place, and having all due knowledge of one another in point of a work of grace on our hearts, religious principles, and moral characters, and being desirous of enjoying the privileges that appertain to the people of God in a church relation, do, in the name of the Lord Jesus:
>
> Voluntarily and freely give ourselves up to the Lord, and to one another, according to his word, to be one body under one head, jointly to exist and act by the bands and rules of the gospel, and do promise and engage to do all things, by divine assistance, in our different capacities and relations that the Lord has commanded us, and requires of us:
>
> - particularly to deny ourselves,
> - take up our cross, follow Christ,
> - keep the faith,
> - assemble ourselves together,
> - love the brethren,
> - submit one to another in the Lord,
> - care one for another,
> - bear one another's burdens,
> - endeavour to keep the unity of the spirit in the bond of peace,
> - and, finally, to honour, obey and maintain them that may have the rule over us in the Lord.
>
> This is the Covenant we solemnly enter into, in the fear of God, humbly imploring the Divine assistance and blessing that we may be built up and established to the glory of God, the advancement of the Redeemer's interest, and

---

27. This covenant is quoted from William H. Brackney (ed.), *Baptist Life and Thought 1600 – 1980: A Sourcebook* (Valley Forge: Judson, 1983), 126.

> the comfort and edification of our own souls, through the infinite riches of free grace, which is in Jesus Christ our Lord: and now, to the only wise God, Father, Son, and Holy Spirit, be worship, honour, power, glory, dominion, and obedience rendered, now and ever more, Amen.

2. A local church glorifies God

We were created to honor God and worship Him in Spirit and in truth. Jesus said His children needed to love Him with everything he had; this was the "great commandment" Jesus quoted from the Old Testament (Deut 6:4-5). He said this was the most important thing a believer could do (Mk 12:29-31). The problem is that, since the Fall, men have followed their own lusts and desires, and pushed God far, far away. The Apostle Paul tells us men don't want to even acknowledge God exists (Rom 1:18-23).

The Bible also tells us that men who are in the flesh cannot please God (Rom 8:8). Only *after* we're called by the Holy Spirit and we become believers can we worship God and "be to the praise of His glory," (Eph 1:12).[28] Salvation restores this broken relationship with God, so that we *can* worship Him.

> *But you are not in the flesh, you are in the Spirit, if in fact the Spirit of God dwells in you. Anyone who does not have the Spirit of Christ does not belong to him. But if Christ is in you, although your bodies are dead because of sin, your spirits are alive because of righteousness.*
>
> *If the Spirit of him who raised Jesus from the dead dwells in you, he who raised Christ Jesus from the dead will give life to*

---

28. Gregg Allison observes, "[t]he situation is reversed for Christians, so that they who 'hope in Christ might be to the praise of his glory' (Eph. 1:12). Jesus himself explained that those who are regenerated by the Holy Spirit are qualified for this doxological purpose," (*Sojourners and Strangers,* KL 2653-2655).

your mortal bodies also through his Spirit which dwells in you (Rom 8:9-11).

And, even when we become believers, we don't do all that good a job of worshipping the Lord. The local church's main job is to please God.[29] We do that by joining together in singing praises to Him, being submissive to the preached word and seeking to have our lives changed to be more like Christ. As the Apostle Paul wrote:

Let the word of Christ dwell in you richly, teach and admonish one another in all wisdom, and sing psalms and hymns and spiritual songs with thankfulness in your hearts to God. And whatever you do, in word or deed, do everything in the name of the Lord Jesus, giving thanks to God the Father through him (Col 3:16-17).

Every Christian should care about this principle, because it means what we do in our local congregations *isn't about us!* It's not about the Pastor(s) being "in charge" and building little empires for themselves. It's also not about you sitting in your favorite pew, or getting upset because Mr. Smith forgot to shake your hand this past Sunday morning. It's not about gossip, whispering, backbiting or cliques or church politics. It's not about how smoothly church events and special functions work (or don't work). It's certainly not about your personal preferences, as if you should shop for a church the way you shop for groceries.

What Christians do in a local church, as a corporate group, is about God. We come to worship Him, and bring Him honor and glory.

---

29. "Therefore, the church's first concern must be to please God. To have a growing church is good; to have a church full of pleased people may be desirable, but the church belongs to God, and the point is pleasing Him," (Hammett, *Biblical Foundations,* 67).

3. A local church is dependent on the Holy Spirit

Christians owe everything to the Holy Spirit, and should be totally *dependent* on the Holy Spirit. He called us and softened our hearts so that we repented and believed. He's the One who helps us grow in our faith.

It was the Spirit who filled the believers, and gave them the supernatural ability to communicate the Gospel in foreign languages, to communicate with the tens of thousands of Jewish pilgrims who were in Jerusalem for Pentecost (Acts 2:1-7). It was the Spirit whom Jesus promised He would send after His ascension back to the Father (see Jn 14:16, 26; cf. Lk 24:49; Acts 1:4). As the Apostle Peter said, "Being therefore exalted at the right hand of God, and having received from the Father the promise of the Holy Spirit, he has poured out this which you see and hear," (Acts 2:33).

The Spirit is the One who indwells sinners when they honestly repent of their sins and believe the Gospel (Acts 2:38 [cf. Jn 14:23]; Acts 8:14-17; 9:14-19; 10:44-46; 11:15-18; 15:8; 19:1-7). It's the Spirit who gives believers unique insight and a supernatural clarity of thought and focus in difficult times (Acts 4:8, 31; 7:55-56; 13:9ff). The Spirit testifies to believers that the Gospel is true (Acts 5:30-32). Christians who are "full of the Spirit" (i.e. controlled by Him) are more spiritually mature (Acts 6:3; 10:22-24). The Spirit strengths Christians in difficult times, and replaces fear with joy (Acts 13:52). The Spirit, behind the scenes, helps Christians make difficult and tough decisions (Acts 15:28).

In short, nobody can read the New Testament without believing that Christians, individually and corporately, are completely dependent on the Holy Spirit. We're called to be controlled by Him. The Apostle Paul's words may be familiar to us, but they're worth quoting in full:

> *But I say, walk by the Spirit, and do not gratify the desires of the flesh. For the desires of the flesh are against the Spirit, and the desires of the Spirit are against the flesh; for these are opposed to each other, to prevent you from doing what you would. But if you are led by the Spirit you are not under the law.*
>
> *Now the works of the flesh are plain: fornication, impurity, licentiousness, idolatry, sorcery, enmity, strife, jealousy, anger, selfishness, dissension, party spirit, envy, drunkenness, carousing, and the like. I warn you, as I warned you before, that those who do such things shall not inherit the kingdom of God.*
>
> *But the fruit of the Spirit is love, joy, peace, patience, kindness, goodness, faithfulness, gentleness, self-control; against such there is no law. And those who belong to Christ Jesus have crucified the flesh with its passions and desires.*
>
> *If we live by the Spirit, let us also walk by the Spirit. Let us have no self-conceit, no provoking of one another, no envy of one another (Gal 5:16-26).*

The Spirit is the One whom Jesus promised to send, as His replacement. Jesus isn't here with His adopted brothers and sisters in bodily form. So He promised He'd sent the Spirit, instead:

> *If you love me, you will keep my commandments. And I will pray the Father, and he will give you another Counselor, to be with you forever, even the Spirit of truth, whom the world cannot receive, because it neither sees him nor knows him; you know him, for he dwells with you, and will be in you (Jn 14:15-17).*

Without the Spirit, we can't grow in personal or corporate holiness, and we can't see anyone come to saving faith. How else will we show the fruits of the Spirit? How else will we grow in the faith? How else can we be holy, because God is holy? How else do we exercise the gifts, talents and abilities God has given us? How else will people we preach the Gospel to even believe?

> *For by one Spirit we were all baptized into one body—Jews or Greeks, slaves or free—and all were made to drink of one Spirit (1 Cor 12:13).*

How else will a church ever have unity?[30] How else will a church ever be able to show to the fruits of the Spirit, as a corporate group? How else will Christians in local churches ever love each other with a pure heart, fervently (1 Pet 1:22)?

We can't rely on ourselves in our daily walk with the Lord, or for anything a local church does. We have to make the daily decision to say "no" to ourselves, pick up our cross, and follow Christ – to walk in the Spirit.

4. A local church focuses on spiritual growth

Church leaders and church members should focus on spiritual growth, not numerical growth.[31] The definition of a "perfect church"

---

30. "As we observed earlier the Spirit, being one, also produces a unity within the body. This does not mean uniformity, but a oneness in aim and action," (Millard J. Erickson, *Christian Theology*, 2nd ed. [Grand Rapids: Zondervan, 1998], 1051).

31. John Hammett writes, "To the degree that the church lives in accord with its own essential being, growth will occur. In some contexts, the growth may be primarily spiritual . . . Certainly the church bore witness to Christ, as He had promised they would (Acts 1:8), but the growth is seen as the work of God. In fact, the teaching of Paul and the pattern of Acts seem to indicate that churches should focus on obedience to Christ's command, 'Follow me;' the results in terms of growth must be entrusted

is one where the church shows the fruits of the Spirit, and grows more and more Christ-like week by week. Perhaps the best "model church" is the congregation in Thessalonica:

> *We give thanks to God always for you all, constantly mentioning you in our prayers, remembering before our God and Father your work of faith and labor of love and steadfastness of hope in our Lord Jesus Christ (1 Thess 1:2-3).*

Paul commended the Thessalonian Christians for their *faith, hope,* and *love,* not for their numbers. No New Testament writer worries about numbers; not one. Instead, the New Testament is worried about a local church's spiritual growth, as a corporate unit. If we can get this right, the rest will fall into place as God wills.

The Apostle Paul didn't commend the Thessalonians for their numbers. Instead, he praises them because the Gospel wasn't just words that passed in one ear, and out the other. Instead, it came in power, in the Holy Spirit, and with full conviction (1 Thess 1:5). They began to imitate Paul, his companions, and the Lord Himself (1 Thess 1:6). They learned from his example, and began to turn from dead idols to serve the living and true God (1 Thess 1:9). Their church became an example to believers throughout the entire region, because "your faith in God has gone forth everywhere," (1 Thess 1:8). They did all this, and patiently waited "for his Son from heaven, whom he raised from the dead, Jesus, who delivers us from the wrath to come," (1 Thess 1:10).

There's nothing here about attendance numbers, social media strategies or tailored music, all calculated to "draw them in." Our job is to be growing as individuals, and this will make our local churches grow spiritually as corporate bodies. Our job is to try our very best to serve God with a pure heart, and leave the results to Him.

---

to Christ, who promised those who follow Him, 'I will make you fishers of men,' (Matthew 4:19)," (*Biblical Foundations,* 73).

God gives the increase, not us (1 Cor 3:5-7). He's in charge of that; we're just responsible to put forth the effort![32] It's very sad that, when you think of a "successful church," the spiritual state of the people is often very last things on people's minds. Instead, the attendance numbers are usually the benchmark we reach for. No, a church's aim should be for spiritual growth, which means a desire to grow in personal and corporate holiness, ongoing discipleship and teaching, a focus on joyful Christian service, and fellowship and mutual support, week after week, month after month.

5. A local church is completely fixated on Christ and the Gospel

The Gospel is why the church is here. The New Covenant in Jesus Christ is the event all of Scripture has been pointing to from the beginning. It's the message God comforted Adam and Eve with after the fall, even as he meted out punishment for their rebellion (Gen 3:15). Jesus is the penultimate "son of Abraham" (Mt 1:1), the One by whom "all the families of the earth shall be blessed," (Gen 12:3).

Jesus is the prophet Moses said would come on the scene; the Israelite who would arise from their own ranks, who'd have a special and unique relationship with Yahweh, who all people who be obligated to listen to (Deut 18:15-19). Jesus is the King the prophet Nathan promised would come from David's lineage, whose kingdom would never end (1 Chr 17:11-15).

Jesus is Yahweh's anointed, the King whom God has set upon His holy hill to rule over His future kingdom (Ps 2). Jesus is the One who sits at Yahweh's right hand even now, and will remain there "till I make

---

32. For further reading on connection between a holy life and our individual obligation to share the Gospel, see Chapter 6, "The Cleansing of the Priests," from Lewis S. Chafer, *True Evangelism* (New York: Gospel Publishing House, 1911), 133-159. "Of this outflow of love it may be stated that, as the love of God is shed abroad in our hearts by the Spirit which is given unto us, the normal experience of every believer should be a Divine sense of the lost condition of unsaved people, which will prompt any necessary sacrifice or effort to win them," (157).

your enemies your footstool," (Ps 110:1). He's the high priest after the order of Melchisidec (Ps 110:4), the "ringer" from outside Aaron's lineage who made perfect and final atonement for all our sins (see all of Hebrews 7). He's the High Priest who can't be defiled by filthy garments stained with sins (Zech 3; cf. Heb 7:26-28).

Jesus is the promised "shoot from the stump of Jesse" (Isaiah 11:2), Yahweh's servant "the Branch" (Zech 3:8), on whom the prophet predicted the Spirit of Yahweh would rest, "the spirit of wisdom and understanding, the spirit of counsel and might, the spirit of knowledge and the fear of the LORD," (Isaiah 11:2). He's the one who came to inaugurate a new and better covenant, "since it is enacted on better promises," (Heb 8:6).

He came preaching the Good News of His coming Kingdom, and commanded everyone everywhere to repent (Mk 1:14-15). He established His divine credentials by casting out demons, raising the dead and healing the sick. Jesus told has astonished hometown crowd in his local synagogue that, just as Isaiah prophesied,

> *The Spirit of the Lord is upon me,*
> *because he has anointed me to preach good news to the poor.*
> *He has sent me to proclaim release to the captives*
> *and recovering of sight to the blind,*
> *to set at liberty those who are oppressed,*
> *to proclaim the acceptable year of the Lord (Lk 4:18-19).*

And, these credentials are the very thing Jesus pointed to when John the Baptist's disciples asked if He was the Messiah (Lk 7:18-23). He's the One who has bound Satan, the strong man, and has plundered his goods by releasing prisoners from the dungeons of sin. As He said:

> *But if it is by the finger of God that I cast out demons, then the kingdom of God has come upon you. When a strong man, fully*

> *armed, guards his own palace, his goods are in peace; but when one stronger than he assails him and overcomes him, he takes away his armor in which he trusted, and divides his spoil (Lk 11:20-22).*

Jesus, by way of this little parable, told us the kingdom of God has broken back into human history through Him. Jesus has bound Satan, and is cheerfully plundering His goods and rescuing sinners from themselves. And, Jesus willingly and voluntarily left the Father's throne room above, and came here to take on a human nature (cf. Phil 2) so that "through death he might destroy him who has the power of death, that is, the devil, and deliver all those who through fear of death were subject to lifelong bondage," (Heb 2:14-15).

Satan has no power over Jesus; He willingly and voluntarily went to His death. "He has no power over me; but I do as the Father has commanded me, so that the world may know that I love the Father. Rise, let us go hence," (Jn 14:30-31). And, even as He was tried before corrupt officials, Jesus explicitly identified Himself as the Messiah and said He would return, just as the prophet Daniel said He would (Mk 14:61-64).

After His death, the Apostle Peter explained,

> *this Jesus, delivered up according to the definite plan and foreknowledge of God, you crucified and killed by the hands of lawless men. But God raised him up, having loosed the pangs of death, because it was not possible for him to be held by it (Acts 2:23-24).*

This happened just as David had said it would, long ago (Ps 16; cf. Acts 2:25-33). Jesus was seen by hundreds of eyewitnesses (1 Cor 15:3-7), proved He bodily rose from the dead in a miraculous fashion, and then rose back to heaven after 40 days (Acts 1:6-11). And, finally, the Bible tells us:[33]

> ... that the end of the world is approaching; that at the last day Christ will descend from heaven, and raise the dead from the grave to final retribution; that a solemn separation will then take place; that the wicked will be adjudged to endless punishment, and the righteous to endless joy; and that this judgment will fix forever the final state of men in heaven or hell, on principles of righteousness.

The Gospel is why God has put us here. It's the "great commission" He gave His disciples at the end of His ministry (Mt 28:19-20). It's the job He gave us to do. That commission is ours, too. The local church's mission is to be about Jesus Christ and His Gospel.

6. A local church is totally committed to the Scriptures

The Bible is where God speaks to us. It's our only infallible authority for Christian faith and practice.[34] The Apostle Paul told Timothy,

> *Follow the pattern of the sound words which you have heard from me, in the faith and love which are in Christ Jesus (2 Tim 1:13)*

---

33. 1833 *New Hampshire Confession of Faith* (Article 18); cited from Lumpkin, *Baptist Confessions,* 367.

34. "Scripture alone is the inerrant, infallible record of God's revelation to mankind. But Scripture is more than the record of God's revelation; it is itself the only inerrant, infallible, inspired revelation from God that exists today . . . The principle of *sola Scriptura* does not claim that the Bible is an exhaustive record of God's special revelation to man, but that it is a sufficient record of all that is *necessary* to be believed for faith and practice," (David T. King, *Holy Scripture: The Pillar and Ground of Our Faith*, 3 vols. [Battle Ground: Christian Resources, 2001], 1:43, 181 [see also pg. 34]).

Paul taught Timothy everything he knows, with a bit of help from his mother and grandmother along the way. Timothy needs to follow Paul's example about "sound words." But Paul is dead, he didn't leave any YouTube videos or mp3 recordings behind for us to find, and Nero unfortunately deleted Paul's FaceBook page. This means the only place we'll find Paul's words, so we can follow them, is in the preserved Word of God – the Bible.

The Bible was written by 40 men, over the course of about 1500 years, and we believe God moved each of those men to record and write exactly what He wanted them to write using their own unique personalities and voice, then preserved these books (through the thousands of copies and their mass distribution, and the reverence God's people have always had for them) down through the centuries so we could have them on our laps, phones, or tablets this coming Sunday.

The Christian story is a worldview, an inter-related network of beliefs and convictions that combine together to inform how we view this world. The Christian faith is a picture and story that interprets reality; that explains "the way things are:"[35]

1. **Creation:** how did we get here?
2. **Fall:** why are things the way they are? Why do bad things happen?

---

35. These days, there are plenty of books which discuss the idea of a Christian worldview. One of the most helpful, I believe, is Gregory Koukl's book *The Story of Reality: How the World Began, How it Ends, and Everything Important that Happens in Between* (Grand Rapids: Zondervan, 2017). His book is really a description of the Christian "story" for seekers; that is, unbelievers who are interested in finding out what Christianity is about. It's a wonderful book to give to someone who fits this description.

My description of the Christian worldview as a "picture" or "story of reality," along with the four "big questions," are taken from his book. Again, I've heard and read this all before, but Koukl did a masterful job of distilling these concepts here.

3. **Redemption:** how can this be fixed? How can things be set right?
4. **Restoration:** will things ever be fixed?

Every worldview, every religion (yes, atheism and scientific naturalism are religions) has a set of beliefs that seek to explain these four, most basic concepts and, together, they form the skeleton people use to interpret and understand the world around them.

The Gospel of Jesus Christ answers each of these four "big questions" in a way no others can (because it's the only truth), and this message has implications that should echo and reverberate throughout every nook, cranny, corner and closet of our personal and corporate lives.

So, when Paul says "follow the pattern of sound words," he means Timothy has to commit himself to preaching and teaching the same message Jesus taught, and Jesus' message is grounded in the Old Testament and all the precious promises it contains.

A church can't be a slave to church traditions that are unbiblical, or be an innovation incubator for misguided leaders who want to "update" the Gospel for today's culture, because we allegedly "know more" than Paul, Peter, John and Jesus did. No, a local church's job is to *translate* the truth accurately from the Bible's original cultural setting to our modern one, not to *transform* that message.[36]

This means a local church (and its leaders) must be committed to following the pattern of sound words we find in the Bible:

1. **a creation** that was made perfect in the beginning, to glorify and honor God;
2. **the rebellion** that ruined everything in the world, including us
3. **God's plan to redeem** and remake Creation, and to save some of us from ourselves along the way, by means of His eternal

---

36. See especially Erickson (*Christian Theology,* 122-129).

son, who lived a perfect life for us in our place and willingly died for our sins in our place as our substitute, and rose from the dead to defeat Satan and the curses of sin and death;

4. **and the promise of glorious restoration** when He comes back one day to defeat all enemies, establish His kingdom, and rule over a new and better creation, and all of us who repent and believe in the Good News will be there with Him, to worship and serve Him for eternity.

God's word is a lamp for our feet, and a light for the paths of life (Ps 119:105). We should treat it that way, too.

7. A local church is looking for Christ's return

Christ's return is the blessed hope of all Christians. It's why we celebrate the Lord's Supper *until Christ comes back* (1 Cor 11:26).

> *For the grace of God has appeared for the salvation of all men, training us to renounce irreligion and worldly passions, and to live sober, upright, and godly lives in this world, awaiting our blessed hope, the appearing of the glory of our great God and Savior Jesus Christ, who gave himself for us to redeem us from all iniquity and to purify for himself a people of his own who are zealous for good deeds (Titus 2:11-14).*

This is what keeps us going day after day.

2: ONLY THE NEW TESTAMENT TELLS US HOW TO "DO CHURCH"

There's a difference between the Old Covenant and the New Covenant.[37] If you want to know the difference, you should read the Book of Hebrews, and have a marker in the Book of Leviticus, too. Here, I'll only focus on one of these differences, which is key to understanding this Baptist distinctive. Here it is:

- **The only place which tells us how to worship God in a New Covenant context is the New Covenant scriptures.**

The New Covenant was inaugurated with Christ's death, burial, resurrection and ascension back to the Father, beginning with the outpouring of the Holy Spirit (Acts 2). It's in effect for the church now, and God will implement it for Israel later, too. The New Covenant wasn't around in the Old Testament; that's why it's "New."

So, Baptists believe our only source for "how to do church" (i.e. polity) is in the New Covenant scriptures. In the New Testament

---

37. I'm a dispensationalist, but it's obvious I'm not arguing that way here. I think the best distinction here is not between the so-called Dispensation of the Law and the Dispensation of Grace, but between the passing away of the Old Covenant and the inauguration of the New. The Covenants are explicitly identified and discussed in the scriptures and all the dispensations are not, so they're a much better framework to hang your theological hat on. This is not the way a dispensational Baptist typically argues for this distinctive.

For an excellent, dispensational Baptist view of the church as God's New Covenant people that actually argues on the basis of covenants (not dispensations), see Allison (*Sojourners and Strangers,* KL 1506 – 2532).

scriptures, God revealed the New Covenant's inauguration and function in the practical life of Christian congregations. So, that means the only place to find out how to "do church" in a New Covenant context is in . . . *(wait for it)* . . . the New Testament.

This immediately sets us apart from most denominations, which often look to the Old Testament for additional insight about how a congregation should function. The Baptists disagree, and this distinctive is the fountainhead from which all the others flow. This is why, for example, a Baptist theologian writing in the 19th century wrote this:[38]

> *As the essential prerequisites for admission to a Christian church are given in the New Testament, no church can rightfully welcome to its fellowship persons who are not believed to have those prerequisites; nor is any church at liberty to insist on qualifications other than those virtually prescribed by the New Testament.*

I'll explain more about this as we move through the rest of the distinctives, below.

---

[38] Alvah Hovey, *Manual of Systematic Theology and Christian Ethics* (Boston: 1877), 304.

3: ONLY PROFESSING CHRISTIANS CAN BE CHURCH MEMBERS

> **SYNOPSIS:**
>
> 1. The promise and fulfillment passages about the New Covenant show it is a covenant only for believers.
> 2. The Old Covenant had two tiers; the first for ethnic Israelities and the second for true believers, who could be Israelites or foreigners who had saving faith and joined God's covenant community. But, the New Covenant *only has one tier* – that of a believer. This presuppositional divide is basic to understanding the difference in interpretation.
> 3. This means only born again, regenerate Christians are members of the local church and the corporate church – His New Covenant community.

This is where the implications of the first distinctive become clear. The Old Covenant membership is different from that of the New Covenant. Here is a famous quotation from the Book of Jeremiah about the New Covenant; pay attention to the bolded section:

> *Behold, the days are coming, says the LORD, when I will make a new covenant with the house of Israel and the house of Judah, not like the covenant which I made with their fathers when I took them by the hand to bring them out of the land of Egypt, my covenant which they broke, though I was their husband, says the LORD.*
>
> *But this is the covenant which I will make with the house of Israel after those days, says the LORD: I will put my law within*

them, and I will write it upon their hearts; and I will be their God, and they shall be my people. **And no longer shall each man teach his neighbor and each his brother, saying, 'Know the LORD,' for they shall all know me, from the least of them to the greatest, says the LORD**; *for I will forgive their iniquity, and I will remember their sin no more (Jeremiah 31:31-34).*

There are a lot of wonderful promises here, of course; but the most important one for our purpose is that **only believers** will be part of this New Covenant. In the New Covenant, there won't be a need to teach covenant people about Yahweh, His grace, His holiness or the Messiah to come; "for they shall all know me." Everybody who is part of the New Covenant will *already* know Him.

How is this possible? Why will all the New Covenant members know Him? Because "I will forgive their iniquity, and I will remember their sin no more." They'll know Yahweh, because He's already forgiven them. So, the text tells us **only believers** will be part of the New Covenant.

The New and Better Covenant

The New Covenant passages teach that this better covenant will be composed of only believers. Here are a few of the more obvious passages:

Ezekiel 11:17-20

This is the end of Ezekiel's terrible vision of the apostasy in Israel. In this passage, God's glory leaves the temple for the last time. It never returned; not after the exile and not even in Jesus' day.

> *Therefore say, 'Thus says the Lord GOD: I will gather you from the peoples, and assemble you out of the countries where you have been scattered, and I will give you the land of Israel.'*
>
> *And when they come there, they will remove from it all its detestable things and all its abominations. And I will give them one heart, and put a new spirit within them; I will take the stony heart out of their flesh and give them a heart of flesh, that they may walk in my statutes and keep my ordinances and obey them; and they shall be my people, and I will be their God.*

God said he'd (1) gather them back to Israel, (2) give them one united heart, (3) give them a new spirit; i.e. the Holy Spirit, (4) give them each a new heart of flesh, so they'll keep and obey His word, and therefore (5) they'll belong to Him. It's clear these people will *all* be believers.

Ezekiel 16:59-63

This passage comes at the end of a depressing allegory, where God compares Israel to both an ungrateful child and to a prostitute of the worst repute.

> *Yea, thus says the Lord GOD: I will deal with you as you have done, who have despised the oath in breaking the covenant, yet I will remember my covenant with you in the days of your youth, and I will establish with you an everlasting covenant.*
>
> *Then you will remember your ways, and be ashamed when I take your sisters, both your elder and your younger, and give*

them to you as daughters, but not on account of the covenant with you.

I will establish my covenant with you, and you shall know that I am the LORD, that you may remember and be confounded, and never open your mouth again because of your shame, when I forgive you all that you have done, says the Lord GOD.

This covenant God promised to establish with the Israelites will be everlasting. The result is that they'll be ashamed and horrified at what they've done. It's a fact that shame and honest remorse accompanies true repentance. They'll know who Yahweh is in a *real, experiential sense.* He'll forgive them for all they've done. These future members of the new covenant will all be believers.

Ezekiel 36:24-31

This promise of the new covenant comes during a long passage where God promises to restore Israel and destroy all enemies:

For I will take you from the nations, and gather you from all the countries, and bring you into your own land. I will sprinkle clean water upon you, and you shall be clean from all your uncleannesses, and from all your idols I will cleanse you.

A new heart I will give you, and a new spirit I will put within you; and I will take out of your flesh the heart of stone and give you a heart of flesh. And I will put my spirit within you, and cause you to walk in my statutes and be careful to observe my ordinances.

You shall dwell in the land which I gave to your fathers; and you shall be my people, and I will be your God. And I will deliver you from all your uncleannesses; and I will summon the grain and make it abundant and lay no famine upon you. I will make the fruit of the tree and the increase of the field abundant, that you may never again suffer the disgrace of famine among the nations.

Then you will remember your evil ways, and your deeds that were not good; and you will loathe yourselves for your iniquities and your abominable deeds.

This passage is similar to Ezekiel 11. God will use water (i.e. the Holy Spirit) to cleanse them from their sin and uncleanness. He'll give them each a new heart and a new spirit, so they'll be able to obey His word. They'll be sorry for their "abominable deeds." This is the baptism of regeneration John the Baptist alluded to; "I baptize you with water, but he will baptize you with the Holy Spirit," (Mk 1:8). It's also the same regeneration Jesus told Nicodemus about; "no one can enter the kingdom of God unless they are born of water and the Spirit," (Jn 3:5).

Zechariah 9:11-12

This passage comes during a great section about the blessings of the future Messianic Kingdom, and the destruction of Israel's enemies. It directly follows the prophesy of Jesus' triumphal entry (Zech 9:9):

As for you also, because of the blood of my covenant with you,
    I will set your captives free from the waterless pit.
Return to your stronghold, O prisoners of hope;
    today I declare that I will restore to you double.

Yahweh says that, because of the blood of His covenant (i.e. His coming new and better covenant), He'll set Israel's captives free from the waterless dungeon they've been trapped in. So, in light of that, God asks them to take heart, because "I will restore to you double!" The point is that these people will *all* be set free. They'll *all* experience the blessings of the new and better covenant.

Hebrews 10:11-22

The Book of Hebrews, in particular, explains God's purpose with the Old Covenant. God found fault with the Israelites; that's why He promised to bring a new and better covenant one day (Heb 8). The writer explained "if that first covenant had been faultless, there would have been no occasion for a second," (Hebrews 9:7). The priestly rituals in the tabernacle (and, later, the temple) were figures, symbols, parables for the present age (Hebrews 9:9).

> *And every priest stands daily at his service, offering repeatedly the same sacrifices, which can never take away sins. But when Christ had offered for all time a single sacrifice for sins, he sat down at the right hand of God, then to wait until his enemies should be made a stool for his feet. For by a single offering he has perfected for all time those who are sanctified. And the Holy Spirit also bears witness to us; for after saying,*
>
> > *"This is the covenant that I will make with them after those days, says the Lord:*
> > *I will put my laws on their hearts,*
> > *and write them on their minds,"*
>
> *then he adds,*
>
> > *"I will remember their sins and their misdeeds no more."*

> *Where there is forgiveness of these, there is no longer any offering for sin. Therefore, brethren, since we have confidence to enter the sanctuary by the blood of Jesus, by the new and living way which he opened for us through the curtain, that is, through his flesh, and since we have a great priest over the house of God, let us draw near with a true heart in full assurance of faith, with our hearts sprinkled clean from an evil conscience and our bodies washed with pure water.*

Christ made a single sacrifice for sins "for all time," and that sacrifice is *tied to the people He made that sacrifice for.* We know this because the texts says, "for by a single offering he has perfected for all time those who are sanctified." The writer then quoted Jeremiah 31, and applied it to the current day. It's clear the New Covenant was intended for believers, and it's only applicable to believers. After all, what business does an unbeliever have marching (figuratively speaking) right through the outer compartment of the temple, casting the veil aside, and bowing down at God's very throne? How can an unbeliever draw near to God in full assurance of faith? How can an unbeliever have his conscience sprinkled clean, and his body washed with pure water?

Contrast Between Covenants

Baptists see a *massive* contrast between the Old and New Covenants. You see, the Old Covenant wasn't composed of believers; it was a mixed covenant:

Old Covenant Membership (Two Tiers)		New Covenant Membership (One Tier)
Tier 1: *Israelites born into the Covenant*	**vs.**	**Tier 1:** *People (Israelites and Gentiles) who repent and believe in Yahweh for salvation*
Tier 2: *People (Israelites and Gentiles) who repent and believe in Yahweh for salvation*		

If an Israelite boy was born to proud parents in Capernaum, then he'd be circumcised as an external sign that he's a member of, and heir to, the Old Covenant promises. Then, he'll (hopefully) be brought up to know, trust, love and believe in Yahweh for salvation. His parents will teach him about Yahweh's grace, love, mercy and kindness (cf. Deut 6:20-25). Hopefully, this boy will grow into a young man who loves Yahweh with all his heart, soul and might (Deut 6:5).

Here's the problem; not every little boy and girl grew up to know, love, trust and believe in Yahweh for salvation. Some did; some didn't. Those who didn't either left the Israelite community entirely, or perhaps "played along" by following the rituals, ceremonies and observing the prescribed festivals in a rote, mindless and empty fashion. The Old Covenant was a mixed multitude. The New Covenant is not.

So, Baptists believe a local New Covenant community (e.g. a church) should only consist of people who are, well . . . members of the New Covenant! You can't be a member of the New Covenant unless you've been "regenerated" (i.e. born again) by the Holy Spirit, and then repented of your rebellion against God and believed in who Jesus is and what He's done.

This is why, for example, the 1833 *New Hampshire Confession of Faith* reads as it does about "a Gospel church" (Article 13):[39]

---

39. Cited from Lumpkin, *Baptist Confessions*, 365 – 366.

> *We believe that a visible Church of Christ **is a congregation of baptized believers, associated by covenant in the faith and fellowship of the gospel** . . .*

In contrast, look at what Presbyterians confess in the 1647 *Westminster Confession of Faith* (Chapter 15):[40]

> **The visible Church**, *which is also catholic or universal under the gospel (not confined to one nation as before under the law)* **consists of all those**, *throughout the world,* **that profess the true religion, and of their children** . . .

The Presbyterians believe the true, visible church *automatically* includes children of believers. They have a two-tiered New Covenant.

The Great Divide

Here is the difference - the Reformed,[41] Presbyterians, the Lutherans[42] and the Anglicans[43] believe children are (in some sense) made part of the New Covenant through the sacrament of baptism. Why do they believe this? There are many reasons, but I'll highlight

---

40. Retrieved from the Center for Reformed Theology and Apologetics, at https://reformed.org/documents/wcf_with_proofs/index.html.

41. See the Belgic Confession (1617), Article 34 and the Westminster Confession of Faith (1647), Chapter 28.

42. Augsburg Confession (1530), Article 9. Cited from Theodore Tappert (ed.), *The Book of Concord: The Confessions of the Evangelical Lutheran Church* (Philadelphia: Fortress, 1959), 33.

43. The 39 Articles of Religion of the Church of England (1562), Article 27. Retrieved from https://www.churchofengland.org/prayer-and-worship/worship-texts-and-resources/book-common-prayer/articles-religion#XXVII.

two of them that are particularly applicable to Reformed churches which follow covenant theology.[44]

First, they believe there is two-tiered parallel between the Old and New Covenants. The Belgic Confession explains (Article 34):

> *Therefore we detest the error of the Anabaptists, who are not content with the one only baptism they have once received, and moreover condemn the baptism of the **infants of believers, who, we believe, ought to be baptized and sealed with the sign of the covenant, as the children in Israel formerly were circumcised upon the same promises which are made unto our children**.*

I'll show you a real-world example:[45]

> ↻ mbird Retweeted
>
> **Anthony Bradley** @drantbradley · 11h
> Huh. Imagine that? When you treat children as covenant children, & not pagans in homes of Christian parents, covenant promises tend to prevail (Deut 6). One of reasons Presbyterians baptize infants & catechize them. The PCA didn't need a study for this;).
>
> **The Gospel Coalition** @TGC
> A new @LifeWayResearch study found that Bible reading in childhood was the best predictor of spiritual health among young adults. thegspl.co/2GjZfw3
>
> ◯ 4   ↻ 15   ♡ 112   ✉

---

44. This systematic framework for interpreting the Bible developed first with John Calvin and was reflected in the Westminster Confession of Faith (1647). It was more formally systematized in the mid to late 17th century by Johannes Cocceius and Francis Turretin. See especially David Beale (*Historical Theology*, 2:69 – 101) for a discussion of the development of Reformed thought in conflict with Arminian theology.

45. This tweet was retrieved from
https://twitter.com/drantbradley/status/957105627473604608.

The Gospel Coalition tweeted the results of a study conducted by LifeWay, the publishing arm of the Southern Baptist Convention. The response, above, is clearly from a Presbyterian, evidently a member of the Presbyterian Church in America (PCA), a conservative denomination. This tweet, in all its glory, sums up this presuppositional divide.

Baptists *do not agree with this at all*. As I discussed above, we see the New Covenant as having one single membership – that of a believer. In contrast, the Old Covenant had two tiers; (1) those ethnic Israelites who were born into it, and (2) those who accepted and believed in Yahweh's promise of a Savior by faith. Baptists believe *everyone* is a pagan unless and until he repents and believes in who Jesus is and what He's done. The Presbyterians, however, believe their children are "born into the covenant," because they have believing parents. So, they seek to encourage their children to "make the faith their own" as they grow.[46] One Reformed theologian remarked, "As long as the children of the covenant do not reveal the contrary, we shall have to proceed on the assumption that they are in possession of the covenant life."[47]

Second, Reformed Christians believe in a covenantal view of salvation that includes both believers and their children. They believe God made a "covenant of grace" with mankind to redeem them, and that every step along the path towards fulfillment through Christ is just a different form of that covenant. So, for example, the covenants with (1) Abraham, (2) Moses and the Israelites, (3) David, and even (4) the New Covenant are just waypoints along the way towards fulfilling the overarching "covenant of grace." As one Reformed confession

---

46. For a good survey of the issue from a Reformed brother, see Michael Horton, *The Christian Faith: A Systematic Theology for Pilgrims on the Way* (Grand Rapids: Zondervan, 2011), 794 – 798.

47. Louis Berkhof, *Systematic Theology,* combined ed. (reprint; Grand Rapids: Eerdmans, 1996), 288.

says, "this covenant was differently administered in the time of the law and in the time of the gospel … there are not, therefore, two covenants of grace differing in substance, but one and the same under various dispensations."[48]

So, because their theological framework is built upon a so-called "covenant of grace" which has changed outward shape periodically throughout the centuries, they believe both children of believers, and even infants who can't exercise saving faith, are part of God's family and "in the covenant." They don't see it as "Old Covenant *vs.* New Covenant." They see it as one overarching "Covenant of Grace."

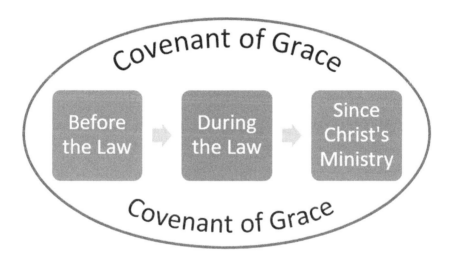

Many Baptists disagree. They see no mention of a so-called "covenant of grace" anywhere in the Bible. They don't believe the passages the Reformed confessions reference have anything to do with a "covenant of grace."[49] Instead, many Baptists believe those oft-

---

48. Westminster Confession of Faith (1647), 7.5, 7.6.

49. Westminster Confession of Faith cites Gal 3:21; Rom 3:20-21; 8:3; Gen 3:15; Isaiah 42:6, Mark 16:15-16; John 3:16; Rom 10:6, 9; Gal 3:11, Ezek 36:26-27; John 6:44-45, Heb 9:15–17; 7:22; Luke 22:20; 1 Cor 11:25 (and more).

cited passages actually describe promises of the new and better covenant in Christ. In short, many (but not all) Baptists completely disagree that there *is* a covenant of grace and reject the covenantal framework altogether.

To be sure, God has had a plan to redeem His creation (including some of us) from eternity past, and the Bible is the story of how God has brought that plan into action through Adam and Eve, Noah, Abraham and the patriarchs, the nation of Israel, the church and (later) the nation of Israel again. He's done all this through His eternal Son, Jesus Christ.

Baptists have many different frameworks for interpreting the Bible. Some are dispensationalists, and reject the framework of covenantal theology.[50] Some are Reformed Baptists who generally follow the covenant framework, but reject the idea that the New Covenant has a mixed membership.[51] But, for every Baptist, this concept of regenerate (i.e. born again) church membership has always been central to a right understanding of the church. It sets us apart from the vast majority of churches in the world today. More than anything else, is it *the* Baptist mark of the church.[52]

---

50. See, for example, Kevin Bauder, *Baptist Distinctives and New Testament Church Order* (Schaumburg: Regular Baptist Press, 2013).

51. See Samuel Waldron and Richard Barcellos, *A Reformed Baptist Manifesto: The New Covenant Constitution of the Church* (Palmdale: RBAP, 2004), 65 – 79.

52. See especially Hammett (*Biblical Foundations,* 81-108).

4: WHO CAN BE BAPTIZED?

> **SYNOPSIS:**
>
> 1. There is a serious presuppositional divide between those, like Baptists, who argue for believer's baptism, and those who argue for infant baptism. Baptists believe *only believers* are members of the New Covenant and, thus, *only believers* can be baptized as an external covenant sign or "mark" that they belong to God.
> 2. In the Old Covenant, the external sign of covenant membership (circumcision) came first, and the internal sign (real saving faith) hopefully came later. But, in the New Covenant, the order is reversed – the internal (baptism of the Spirit) comes first and the external (believer's baptism) is second.
> 3. The New Testament evidence shows believer's baptism pictures the baptism of the Holy Spirit, and thus symbolizes a new believer's death to sin by union with Christ's death, and his spiritual birth by union with Christ's resurrection.
> 4. The New Testament evidence shows that believer's baptism pictures a once for all washing and total cleansing from sin.
> 5. The New Testament evidence shows that believer's baptism pictures a new believer joining the New Covenant community, and being made part of the corporate body of Christ by union with His death and resurrection.

Baptists believe only believers should be baptized, because the New Covenant only includes believers. The 1833 *New Hampshire Confession of Faith* reads (Article 14):[53]

> *We believe that Christian Baptism is the **immersion in water of a believer**, into the name of the Father, and Son, and Holy Ghost; **to show forth, in a solemn and beautiful emblem, our***

---

53. Cited from Lumpkin, *Baptist Confessions,* 366.

faith in the crucified, buried, and risen Saviour, *with its effect in our death to sin and resurrection to a new life; that it is prerequisite to the privileges of a Church relation . . .*

As one Baptist has written, believer's baptism "symbolizes the regeneration of the subject, as being, on the one hand, a dying to sin, and, on the other, a rising to holiness."[54]

This conviction flows from our presupposition that the New Covenant scriptures are the only place which tells us how we, a New Covenant people, ought to worship God as a congregation. And, in the New Testament, we believe the Bible only shows us *believers* being baptized, and by immersion. As the 1689 *London Baptist Confession of Faith* reads, "Those who do actually profess repentance towards God, faith in, and obedience to, our Lord Jesus Christ, are the only proper subjects of this ordinance."[55]

Robert Reymond, a Reformed theologian and Presbyterian who argued for infant baptism, presented some good arguments that represent the best the other side has. He believed infants should be baptized for three reasons:[56]

1. Infant males received the covenant sign of circumcision under the Old Covenant
2. The covenant of grace has a continuity which makes the "people of God" one, in every age
3. There is no command to repeal the practice of placing a covenant sign on covenant children, today. He explained, "as a biblical principle ... the sacramental continuity between the

---

54. Hovey, *Systematic*, 321.

55. *London Baptist Confession of Faith* (1689), Article 29, §2.

56. Reymond (*Systematic*, 944).

testaments is so strong that *not* to baptize children of believers would require some explicit word of repeal."[57]

There is really just one basic objection here; a disagreement over who is eligible to be a New Covenant member.

The Presuppositional Divide

There is a lot of good material available about the "baptism issue."[58] For our purposes, it's enough that you realize our conviction on this point flows from the following:

1. The New Covenant scriptures are the only place where *New Covenant* members learn how to worship Yahweh in a *New Covenant* context, and
2. There is a marked contrast between the two-tiered Old Covenant (believers *and* unbelievers), and the one-tiered New Covenant (believers only).

Both the Old and New Covenants have external signs and internal signs, which signify covenant membership.

Under the Old Covenant, the "external sign" of covenant membership was circumcision. Eventually, parents hoped their child would "circumcise their heart" (this is regeneration; cf. Deut 10:16; Jeremiah 4:4, etc.) and follow God's law out of loving obedience and allegiance to Yahweh, by faith. *Note the order* – the external is first (for children; i.e. unbelievers), and the internal (actual fidelity based on love for Yahweh) will *hopefully* follow one day.

---

57. Reymond (*Systematic,* 936).

58. A good, fair and honest discussion of the Baptist view on the ordinance is in Erickson (*Christian Theology,* 1098 – 1114).

Under the New Covenant, the order is completely reversed; *the external rite follows the internal regeneration.*

Old Covenant Signs of Membership - in Order		New Covenant Signs of Membership - in Order
#1 - **External:** *Circumcision*	vs.	#1 - **Internal:** *Baptism of the Spirit (i.e. regeneration)*
#2 - **Internal:** *Circumcision of the heart (i.e. regeneration)*		#2 - **External:** *Believer's baptism (i.e. solemn commitment rite to Yahweh and the congregation)*

The New Covenant internal covenant sign is the baptism by the Holy Spirit;[59] that act of God's grace that produces regeneration and gives "a holy disposition to the mind," and "is effected in a manner above our comprehension by the power of the Holy Spirit, in connection with divine truth, so as to secure our voluntary obedience to the gospel."[60]

The New Covenant's external sign is *believer's baptism,* which is the outward rite that shows, tells and marks our God-given faith in Jesus Christ. It's a commitment ceremony, where the new believer confesses to Yahweh and the congregation he's joining that God has indeed forgiven his sin, and remembers his iniquity no more.[61]

This is a serious doctrinal divide, and it's a shame many Christians today don't take doctrine more seriously. What is the nature of the New Covenant, which our Lord and Savior inaugurated so long ago? One General Baptist confession from 1660 explains baptism is only for

---

59. See especially the discussion about the different views of the meaning of baptism by Erickson (*Christian Theology,* 1099 – 1110). "If anything has taken the place of external circumcision, then, it is not baptism but internal circumcision," (1109). Likewise, Larry Oats observed, "Ontologically, baptism signifies the presence of the Holy Spirit already in the believer," (unpublished class notes, GPA 614 – Baptist Polity [Watertown: Maranatha Baptist Seminary, 2013]).

60. *New Hampshire Confession of Faith* (1833), Article 7.

61. On the meaning of believer's baptism, see Hammet (*Biblical Foundations,* 263ff).

those who "profess repentance towards God, and faith towards our Lord Jesus Christ." It went on:[62]

> *And as for all such who preach not this Doctrine, but instead thereof, that Scriptureless thing of Sprinkling of infants (false called Baptisme) whereby the pure word of God is made of no effect, and the new Testament-way of bringing in Members, into the church by regeneration, cast out . . . all such we utterly deny, foreasmuch as we are commanded to have no fellowship with the unfruitful works of darkness, but rather to reprove them.*

However, Robert Reymond (our Presbyterian, Reformed friend) is representative of the infant baptism camp when he assumes a continuity in covenant status. He doesn't see a *two-tiered* Old Covenant of believers and unbelievers, coupled with a *single-tiered* New Covenant of only believers. He sees *both* covenants as two-tiered. He believed the New Covenant can contain unbelievers!

This is why he claimed, "the church should baptize its infants because God requires that covenant children be baptized and for no other reason."[63] And, "[t]he Old Testament practice of reckoning children among the covenant people of God and having the covenant sign administered to them in infancy is nowhere repealed in the New Testament."[64]

We already discussed the nature of New Covenant membership (see ch. 3). Here, we'll look at the Scriptures and see for ourselves who baptism is for, and who it isn't.

---

62. William L. Lumpkin, "The Standard Confession (1660)," in *Baptist Confessions of Faith*, revised ed. (Valley Forge: Judson, 1969), Article 11.

63. Reymond (*Systematic*, 939).

64. Reymond (*Systematic*, 940).

What Does Baptism Mean?

The Book of Acts shows that only believers are baptized, and that the ordinance symbolizes and pictures what the Spirit has done to the new believer. The best way to see this for yourself is to read the New Testament carefully (especially the Book of Acts). Keep a pad of paper handy, and note every time a person is baptized. Is he a believer? What are the circumstances of this baptism? What does it seem to mean?

Here, I'll provide a brief discussion of every relevant passage in the New Testament about baptism from the Book of Acts onward,[65] but I urge the reader to study this for himself.

Acts 2:37-41

This passage comes at the end of Peter's famous Pentecost sermon:

> *Now when they heard this they were cut to the heart, and said to Peter and the rest of the apostles, "Brethren, what shall we do?"*
>
> *And Peter said to them, "Repent, and be baptized every one of you in the name of Jesus Christ for the forgiveness of your sins; and you shall receive the gift of the Holy Spirit. For the promise is to you and to your children and to all that are far off, every one whom the Lord our God calls to him.*

---

65. I'm starting with the Book of Acts, because the New Covenant was inaugurated with the outpouring of the Holy Spirit after Jesus' ascension.

> *And he testified with many other words and exhorted them, saying, "Save yourselves from this crooked generation."* ***So those who received his word were baptized****, and there were added that day about three thousand souls.*

It's clear those who were baptized by the church were believers. They'd "received his word" in the sense that they'd done what Peter recommended; they'd repented and were *then* baptized. God had forgiven their sins, and they'd received the gift of the Holy Spirit.

Some people claim that, because Peter said, "the promise is to you and to your children," that Peter encouraged infants to be baptized.[66] Baptists disagree, and believe Peter was simply saying the promise of forgiveness was for everyone. That is, the promise is for them, their children, those who are far away – everyone whom God calls!

Regardless, the only people who were baptized that day were "those who received his word." Baptism is for believers

Acts 8:12-13

In this passage, the deacon Phillip preaches the Gospel in Samaria, among the people whom Simon the magician had deceived:

> *But **when they believed** Philip as he preached good news about the kingdom of God and the name of Jesus Christ**, they were baptized, both men and women. Even Simon himself believed, and after being baptized** he continued with Philip. And seeing signs and great miracles performed, he was amazed.*

---

66. Reymond wrote, "[t]his Peterine declaration assures us that the ancient promise that embraced children along with their parents continues unabated in this age," (*Systematic,* 941).

The people in Samaria were only baptized *after* they believed. This was true even for Simon, the magician! The ordinance follows belief, and so baptism is for believers.

Acts 8:34-38

This is the end of Luke's account of the deacon Philip preaching to the Ethiopian man who'd been reading the prophesy from Isaiah:

> *And the eunuch said to Philip, "About whom, pray, does the prophet say this, about himself or about some one else?" Then Philip opened his mouth, and beginning with this scripture he told him the good news of Jesus.*
>
> *And as they went along the road they came to some water, and the eunuch said, "See, here is water!* **What is to prevent my being baptized?"** *And he commanded the chariot to stop, and they both went down into the water, Philip and the eunuch,* **and he baptized him.**

The Bible doesn't specifically say this Ethiopian man repented and believed the Gospel, but the context certainly suggests it! Again, the man was only baptized *after* he'd heard the Gospel, and the deacon Philip then baptized him.

Acts 10:44-48

This is the last bit of Luke's account of the conversion of Cornelius and those in his household:

> *While Peter was still saying this, the Holy Spirit fell on all who heard the word. And the believers from among the circumcised who came with Peter were amazed, because the gift of the*

> *Holy Spirit had been poured out even on the Gentiles. For they heard them speaking in tongues and extolling God.*
>
> *Then Peter declared,* **"Can any one forbid water for baptizing these people who have received the Holy Spirit just as we have?" And he commanded them to be baptized in the name of Jesus Christ.** *Then they asked him to remain for some days.*

The Holy Spirit came upon and regenerated everyone who had heard Peter speak. They'd heard the story of salvation (Acts 10:34-43), that "to him all the prophets bear witness that every one who believes in him receives forgiveness of sins through his name," (Acts 10:43). They'd believed that message, received the gift of the regenerating Spirit, and the Israelites who'd accompanied Peter were astonished that God would show grace to Gentiles!

This miniature Gentile Pentecost wasn't what their exclusivist upbringing had taught them to expect from the Lord, even though the Old Covenant scriptures had always commanded them to show love to the Gentiles who joined God's covenant community (see, for example, Isaiah 56).

Peter's first thought is to baptize these new believers. Why? Because they'd "received the Holy Spirit just as we have," (Acts 10:47). So, these new believers were baptized.

Acts 16:14-15

This is from Luke's first-hand account of a missionary journey with the Apostle Paul in the city of Philippi:

> *One who heard us was a woman named Lydia, from the city of Thyatira, a seller of purple goods, who was a worshiper of God. The Lord opened her heart to give heed to what was said by Paul.* **And when she was baptized,** *with her household, she*

> besought us, saying, "If you have judged me to be faithful to the Lord, come to my house and stay." And she prevailed upon us.

The Lord opened Lydia's heart so she'd listen to and receive the Gospel. After she believed, Paul baptized her *along with* her household. The text doesn't say there were infants in the house. It just says the people in her household were baptized, along with Lydia. It's hard to imagine Paul baptizing people who were still unbelievers, especially when all the other passages show only believers being baptized. Even in Cornelius' case, his household joined him in honestly repenting and believing the Gospel. There's no reason to assume this *isn't* what happened for Lydia household, too.

And, for extra support that this was the normal way of things, see the account of the Philippian jailer (Acts 16:25-34, also below). Again, baptism is for believers.

Acts 16:29-34

While still in Philippi, Paul conducted an exorcism on a Gentile slave woman. Her owners were enraged, and Paul and Silas were arrested and beaten by a mob, then thrown into prison. This is the account of the Philippian jailer's conversion:

> And he called for lights and rushed in, and trembling with fear he fell down before Paul and Silas, and brought them out and said, "Men, what must I do to be saved?" And they said, "Believe in the Lord Jesus, and you will be saved, you and your household." And they spoke the word of the Lord to him and to all that were in his house.
>
> And he took them the same hour of the night, and washed their wounds, **and he was baptized at once, with all his**

family. *Then he brought them up into his house, and set food before them; and he rejoiced with all his household that he had believed in God.*

This is a wonderful account! The jailer asks how he can be saved from his sins. Paul tells him to believe in the Lord Jesus Christ, "you and your household," (Acts 16:31). That last bit further explains the command to believe, as if to say, "you'll be saved if you believe in Jesus Christ; both you *and* your household need to do this and you'll *all* be saved!"

So, Paul and Silas preached "to him and to all that were in his house," (Acts 16:32). What happened next? He and his family were baptized, and his household rejoiced with him because "he had believed in God," (Acts 16:34). It's important to remember that "all his household" was happy for the jailer, yet infants can't rejoice about this at all![67] Baptism is for believers.

Acts 18:8

> *Crispus, the ruler of the synagogue, believed in the Lord, together with all his household; and many of the Corinthians hearing Paul* **believed and were baptized.**

This account is interesting, because we see Paul once again *immediately* move on from a new convert to evangelize that new Christian's household. This is what happened with Lydia, and with the Philippian jailer. But, the important point here is that many

---

67. "Verse 34 offers an important piece of evidence that is often missed for interpreting this passage. It says the entire household 'rejoiced.' Such rejoicing is only possible for those who understood the significance and meaning of what had just happened, which would not include infants," (Thomas Schreiner, "Baptism in the Bible," in *Baptist Foundations: Church Government for an Anti-Institutional Age* [Nashville: B&H, 2015; Kindle ed.], KL 1989-1991).

Corinthians believed the Gospel *and then* were baptized. Baptism is for believers.

Acts 19:1-7

> *While Apollos was at Corinth, Paul passed through the upper country and came to Ephesus. There he found some disciples. And he said to them, "Did you receive the Holy Spirit when you believed?"*
>
> *And they said, "No, we have never even heard that there is a Holy Spirit." And he said, "Into what then were you baptized?"*
>
> *They said, "Into John's baptism." And Paul said, "John baptized with the baptism of repentance, telling the people to believe in the one who was to come after him, that is, Jesus."*
>
> *On hearing this, they were baptized in the name of the Lord Jesus. And when Paul had laid his hands upon them, the Holy Spirit came on them; and they spoke with tongues and prophesied. There were about twelve of them in all.*

These people in Ephesus were disciples of John the Baptist, and hadn't realized the promised Messiah had already come and gone! Who knows how they'd heard John's message; perhaps some of them were in the area during his ministry and carried the message back to Ephesus. So, they'd been waiting for something that had already happened. The Messiah had already come, bringing the baptism of the Holy Spirit (see Mk 1:8).

They believed in Christ, according to the revelation they had at the time. Paul knew this and accepted it; it's why he asked them, "did you receive the Holy Spirit when you believed?" (Acts 19:2). But, he wanted them to know their waiting was over. So, he gave them proper

Christian baptism *because they were already believers.* Baptism is for believers.

Acts 22:16

Here, Paul is recounting his salvation experience, and explaining what Ananias told him to do:

> *And now why do you wait?* **Rise and be baptized**, *and wash away your sins, calling on his name.*

Paul says Ananias told him to do two things, (1) get up and be baptized, and (2) wash away his sins by calling on Jesus' name. Many English translations don't want to be dogmatic here because baptism is a contentious issue. But, the context clearly supports translating this as, "wash away your sins **by** calling on His name."[68] The NIV and William Tyndale, the first man to translate the New Testament into English, understood it this way. So do several commentators.

This short survey from the Book of Acts shows that baptism is an ordinance only for believers. This is because the New Covenant only includes believers, and the external sign and badge of that membership is believer's baptism.

Romans 6:1-11

This passage is perhaps the most important passage in the New Testament about baptism. Paul has just explained that, although Adam's sins made us all sinners, "so one man's act of righteousness leads to acquittal and life for all men. For as by one man's

---

68. The Greek text is ἀναστὰς βάπτισαι καὶ ἀπόλουσαι τὰς ἁμαρτίας σου ἐπικαλεσάμενος τὸ ὄνομα αὐτοῦ. The command is to "wash your sins." How can Paul do this? The adverbial participle explains *how* to do this; Paul must "call upon His name."

disobedience many were made sinners, so by one man's obedience many will be made righteous," (Rom 5:18-19). Wherever sin exists, God's grace abounds much more (Rom 5:20)!

So, should Christians continue sinning, so God's grace would be poured out more and more (Rom 6:1)? Of course not (Rom 6:2)! Paul goes on to make a very critical point; baptism is a picture of a spiritual reality. If we've died to sin, how can be go on living in it day by day (Rom 6:2)? After all, those who have been baptized into union with Christ and been made one with Him[69] have also, by default, been baptized into union with His death, too (Rom 6:3). Christians have been made one with Christ, and just as He died to sins and then walked in newness of life, believers must imitate their Savior's example (Rom 6:4). Just as Christ was buried, we, too, have been figuratively "buried therefore with Him by baptism into death," (Rom 6:4). This is a spiritual union, and it refers to an invisible but objective reality that happens when the Spirit baptizes you into Christ's family. "For if we have been united with him in a death like his, we shall certainly be united with him in a resurrection like his," (Rom 6:5).

Our old person was crucified and put to death in union with Christ, so that we'd be set free from the chains of sin (Rom 6:6). "For he who has died is freed from sin," (Rom 6:7). But, just as Christ died then rose again, our old self has died and our new person in Christ has risen from its spiritual grave (Rom 6:8); we've been born again! Death has no hold on Jesus, and He proved that by His resurrection (Rom 6:9).

Jesus made a clean, decisive, "once for all" break with sin and destroyed it (Rom 6:10). The writer of Hebrews told us Jesus did this so that, "through death he might destroy him who has the power of death, that is, the devil, and deliver all those who through fear of

---

69. For this view, see Douglas J. Moo, *The Epistle to the Romans* in NICNT (Grand Rapids: Eerdmans, 1996) 359 - 365 and John Murray, *The Epistle to the Romans,* combined ed., in NICNT (Grand Rapids: Eerdmans, 1968), 214 – 215. The explanatory thrust of Romans 6:5 (γάρ) makes it clear, I believe, that union with Christ's death and resurrection life is the overriding theme in the baptism picture.

death were subject to lifelong bondage," (Heb 2:14-15). Jesus died to sin, but now "the life he lives he lives to God," (Rom 6:10).

So, what's Paul's point? It's simple; "so you also must consider yourselves dead to sin and alive to God in Christ Jesus," (Rom 6:11). He then went on and exhorted the church at Rome to not let sin "reign in your mortal bodies, to make you obey their passions," (Rom 6:12). After all, God has set them free from all that (Rom 6:13). Now, they can be servants of righteousness, "for sin will have no dominion over you, since you are not under law but under grace," (Rom 6:14). After all, the Apostle continued, "now that you have been set free from sin and have become slaves of God, the return you get is sanctification and its end, eternal life," (Rom 6:22).

This passage tells us that, because Christ has set us free from sin and given us resurrection life, we *can* and *must* "walk in newness of life" and not be slaves to our sins anymore. The instrument who accomplished all this was the Holy Spirit, who baptized us into union with Christ's death, and then raised us into union with Him in His resurrection. "For if we have been united with him in a death like his, we shall certainly be united with him in a resurrection like his," (Rom 6:5).

These are spiritual realities, and they're pictured in a beautiful way by the ordinance of baptism. When we put the candidate under the water, we symbolize and picture the new believer's death to self and union with Christ. When we raise the candidate up out of the water, we show how the Spirit gave him spiritual life, united him into Christ's resurrection, and enabled him to walk in newness of life. Years ago, I made these silly illustrations to explain to children (and adults!) what believer's baptism symbolizes:

Jesus Died = Your Old, Sinful Person Died

Jesus Buried = Your Old Person is Buried and Gone

Jesus' Resurrection = Your New Birth and Spiritual Resurrection!

1 Corinthians 1:13-16

This is at the beginning of the letter, where Paul upbraids the church for playing favorites with their leaders:

> *Is Christ divided? Was Paul crucified for you? Or were you baptized in the name of Paul? I am thankful that I baptized none of you except Crispus and Gaius; lest any one should say that you were baptized in my name. (I did baptize also the household of Stephanas. Beyond that, I do not know whether I baptized any one else).*

These are people who Paul told us are sanctified and called to be saints (1 Cor 1:1). They're believers. It's clear Paul understood the ordinance of baptism was for believers, because he discusses whom he baptized at this church.

1 Corinthians 6:9-11

In this passage, Paul is criticizing the Corinthians for their unholy personal conduct:

> *Do you not know that the unrighteous will not inherit the kingdom of God? Do not be deceived; neither the immoral, nor idolaters, nor adulterers, nor sexual perverts, nor thieves, nor the greedy, nor drunkards, nor revilers, nor robbers will inherit the kingdom of God. And such were some of you. But you were* **washed, you were sanctified, you were justified** *in the name of the Lord Jesus Christ and in the Spirit of our God.*

Paul is using water metaphors to refer to the Holy Spirit, and the way He saves sinners. We're washed in clean water and cleansed from all our sins (Ezek 36:25). Jesus sends the Spirit, who baptizes or *immerses* us in God's grace (Mk 1:8). We're sanctified and declared holy as a result, and justified before God because of what Christ has done for us. This is about the baptism of the Holy Spirit which, as we saw in Romans 6, is the spiritual reality that the ordinance of believer's baptism pictures.

1 Corinthians 12:12-13

Here, Paul discusses spiritual gifts. He made sure to tell the Corinthian church that "to each is given the manifestation of the Spirit for the common good," (1 Cor 12:7). Each person is gifted differently, but every believer is part of the one body of Christ:

> *For just as the body is one and has many members, and all the members of the body, though many, are one body, so it is with Christ.* **For by one Spirit we were all baptized into one body—**

> *Jews or Greeks, slaves or free—and all were made to drink of one Spirit.*

This is the same imagery that Paul used in Romans 6; the Spirit baptizes and immerses every sinner into union with Christ when he repents and believes. We're all part of the corporate church, and we're each important to the Lord, "for the body does not consist of one member but of many," (1 Cor 12:14).

Galatians 3:23-27

Here, Paul contrasts the purpose of the Mosaic law with the fulfillment that Christ brought in the new and better covenant:

> *Now before faith came, we were confined under the law, kept under restraint until faith should be revealed. So that the law was our custodian until Christ came, that we might be justified by faith. But now that faith has come, we are no longer under a custodian; for in Christ Jesus you are all sons of God, through faith.* **For as many of you as were baptized into Christ have put on Christ.**

The Mosaic law acted as a set of guardrails, restraining sinners until Christ would come. It was our "custodian." But, now that Christ has come, the custodian isn't needed any longer. The ceremonial and civil laws that regulated the Israelite society are done away with, because Christ fulfilled those types and shadows. Now, everybody who has faith in Jesus is a "son of God." Why is that? Because, Paul explained, anyone who has been baptized into union with Christ has clothed himself with Him!

Again, Paul is speaking about the baptism of the Holy Spirit, who baptizes sinners into union with Christ's death and raises them to spiritual resurrection. This is the spiritual, inward reality which the ordinance of believer's baptism shows and tells to the congregation and to the world.

Ephesians 4:1-6

In this passage, Paul exhorted the congregation at Ephesus to have patience and kindness towards one another. He points to what unites them:

> *I therefore, a prisoner for the Lord, beg you to lead a life worthy of the calling to which you have been called, with all lowliness and meekness, with patience, forbearing one another in love, eager to maintain the unity of the Spirit in the bond of peace. There is one body and one Spirit, just as you were called to the one hope that belongs to your call, one Lord, one faith, **one baptism**, one God and Father of us all, who is above all and through all and in all.*

Different Christians argue about which baptism is implied here; baptism of the Spirit or the ordinance? I believe it's the baptism of the Spirit. But, for our purposes here it doesn't really matter; it's enough to think about what Paul is saying. He wrote it to people he knew were believers. We know this because he addressed it to the "saints who are also faithful in Christ Jesus," (Eph 1:1). And, he reminded them of what they had in common; they'd been called to the Gospel by God and shared the same Lord, the same faith, the same baptism (however you wish to interpret it), and the same God and Father.

This is obviously a letter written to professing believers, and Paul reminded them of the spiritual or physical baptism they shared. Baptism is for believers, no matter which way you slice it.

Colossians 2:8-15

> *See to it that no one makes a prey of you by philosophy and empty deceit, according to human tradition, according to the elemental spirits of the universe, and not according to Christ. For in him the whole fulness of deity dwells bodily, and you have come to fulness of life in him, who is the head of all rule and authority.*
>
> *In him also you were **circumcised with a circumcision made without hands, by putting off the body of flesh in the circumcision of Christ; and you were buried with him in baptism, in which you were also raised with him through faith in the working of God, who raised him from the dead. And you, who were dead in trespasses and the uncircumcision of your flesh, God made alive together with him,** having forgiven us all our trespasses, having canceled the bond which stood against us with its legal demands; this he set aside, nailing it to the cross. He disarmed the principalities and powers and made a public example of them, triumphing over them in him.*

Paul warned the church at Colossae to follow Christ, and not the mystical, incipient gnostic speculations of unbelievers. Believers have experienced a circumcision "made without hands." What is this mysterious circumcision? Whatever it is, Paul explained that it put to death their old person by Christ's circumcision, buried them with Christ in baptism, and then raised them up with Christ through faith. Through this "circumcision," God made them alive together with Christ, forgave them of all their sins and cancelled the debt which stood against them.

This "circumcision" is inward; it's the baptism of the Holy Spirit. Just as the external rite of circumcision outwardly marked Israelite boys and men who belonged to Yahweh, so the *inward rite* of spiritual circumcision marks everyone who belongs to Yahweh in the new and better covenant. In the Old Testament, Moses used the same analogy of *inward circumcision* to refer to a heart oriented towards God; "circumcise therefore the foreskin of your heart, and be no longer stubborn," (Deut 10:16).

In this passage from Colossians, Paul used the same "baptism" metaphors here that he did in Romans 6. Believer's baptism is an external ordinance for the new believer, which symbolizes and pictures an inward, spiritual reality to the congregation.

Titus 3:3-7

This passage is prompted by Paul's advice to Titus to exhort his congregation to be kind to one another. In many ways, it parallels Ephesians 4:1-5:

> *For we ourselves were once foolish, disobedient, led astray, slaves to various passions and pleasures, passing our days in malice and envy, hated by men and hating one another; but when the goodness and loving kindness of God our Savior appeared, he saved us, not because of deeds done by us In righteousness, but in virtue of his own mercy,* **by the washing of regeneration and renewal in the Holy Spirit, which he poured out upon us richly through Jesus Christ our Savior, so that we might be justified by his grace and become heirs** *in hope of eternal life.*

How are Christians saved? They're saved by the washing of regeneration and renewal in the Holy Spirit. He washes sinners clean from all their sins, and the Spirit is dispensed and poured out upon us richly by Jesus (cf. Acts 2:33), and as a result we're justified by His grace. This is yet another metaphor for the Spirit baptizing, immersing and washing us from our sins and making us new.

Hebrews 10:19-22

This passage comes after a long, beautiful discussion of Jesus as the great, perfect and final High Priest, from the order of Melchisidec:

> *Therefore, brethren, since we have confidence to enter the sanctuary by the blood of Jesus, by the new and living way which he opened for us through the curtain, that is, through his flesh, and since we have a great priest over the house of God, let us draw near with a true heart in full assurance of faith, with **our hearts sprinkled clean from an evil conscience and our bodies washed with pure water**.*

This is another water metaphor which describes the Spirit washing and regenerating sinner's hearts. Here, the writer says believer's hearts have been "sprinkled clean from an evil conscience," which is a clear allusion to blood atonement from the Old Covenant law. Also, their bodies have been "washed with pure water." This water cleanses them, and it's also perfectly pure. This is the baptism of the Holy Spirit, which washed their sins away.

1 Peter 3:19-22[70]

This passage is a short rabbit-trail Peter followed after describing the mindset Christ showed during His ministry:

> *After that, He then went and made proclamation to the spirits [now] in prison, who did not obey in the past when God kept waiting patiently during Noah's days, when the boat was being built in which a few souls (that is, eight) were saved by means*

---

70. This is my own translation.

of water, which also corresponds to **the baptism that has now saved you.**

[This baptism] isn't a removal of filth from the body, but an appeal to God for a good conscience, because of the resurrection of Jesus Christ. *He's at the right hand of God, having gone into heaven, with angels, authorities and powers subject to Him.*

This is a very, very hotly disputed passage. Sacramentalists believe it teaches that the ordinance of baptism actually saves a sinner. Some Baptists believe it describes the ordinance also, but argue this doesn't imply it saves anybody. I believe a better and simpler way is to see this as describing the baptism of the Holy Spirit. The ordinance of baptism has never saved anybody, so Peter must be referring to the baptism of the Spirit.

Peter's point is that, just as the floodwaters were how Noah and his family were saved from the wickedness of the world, the baptism of the Spirit is how God rescues us, washes us clean, "and deliver[s] us from this present, evil world," (Gal 1:4, KJV). This baptism isn't an external thing, like washing dirt from your body; it's a spiritual, internal thing. It's an appeal to God to be free of the guilt and consciousness of our own sin, to finally have a good conscience before God, and an appeal for salvation which results in the new birth, where our sins are washed away. And, don't forget, this salvation is only possible "because of the resurrection of Jesus Christ," (see Acts 2:22-36; esp. v. 33).

The analogy of Noah's floodwaters to the Spirit's baptism also implies something like a deluge or, shall we say, a flood!?

Summary of Baptism

From this long survey, we can draw some general conclusions about who the ordinance is for and what it means:

1. The ordinance is for believers who have been made members of the New Covenant
2. Believer's baptism pictures the baptism of the Holy Spirit, and thus symbolizes and shows a new believer's death to sin by union with Christ's death, and spiritual birth by union with Christ's resurrection
3. Because the ordinance also pictures and symbolizes the baptism (i.e. immersion) by the Holy Spirit, it also shows and symbolizes a once for all washing and total cleansing from sins
4. Believer's baptism symbolizes and pictures a new believer joining the New Covenant community, and being made part of the body of Christ by union with His death and resurrection.

Christians who believe and teach infant baptism are sincere, and love the Lord. They're just wrong, on this point.

5: HOW IS BAPTISM DONE?

> **SYNOPSIS:**
>
> 1. The Greek word "baptize" usually (but not always) implies an immersion or a dipping, in context. It can also mean *washing,* in a more generic sense.
> 2. The Old Testament promises about the New Covenant baptism of the Spirit describe a divine "washing from sins" with vivid metaphors of *pouring* and *cleansing*.
> 3. The New Testament fulfillment of this imagery is described as the Spirit *clothing* believers, *falling* on them, *filling* them and being *poured out* upon them. Immersion in believer's baptism best captures the imagery of all these metaphors; a dainty sprinkling or pouring won't fit the bill.
> 4. The Old Testament imagery of *sprinkling* from sins in Ezekiel (et al) is about Jesus' work of atonement, not the Spirit's work in applying these benefits to the new believer. The atonement concept is expressed by the object lessons of the Lord's Supper.
> 5. The imagery from Romans 6 about Spirit baptism and its results for the new believer is best expressed by immersion, not sprinkling or pouring.

Why should baptism be by immersion? Baptists have traditionally advanced five arguments:[71]

---

71. In my view, these five reasons are the most common. For a longer argument, see especially Adoniram Judson, *Christian Baptism* (Kindle reprint; GLH Publishing, 2017), available at https://amzn.to/2USL2ge.

    See also the sermon by a Baptist named Henry Weston, Pastor of Madison Avenue Baptist Church, NY, who delivered a conference lecture in 1867 entitled, "Baptism – A Symbol."

    In the lecture, he identified five things which baptism symbolized; (1) confession of sin, which is an acknowledgment of uncleanness and spiritual death, (2) the new birth, which is new life in Christ characterized by purity and imputed righteousness, (3)

1. The very word "baptism" usually means "immersion," in context;
2. A contextual study of "baptism" in scripture implies immersion (e.g. "and when he came **up out of** the water," Mk 1:10);
3. Baptism symbolizes and pictures the fact of the new birth, which is the death of the old man and the regeneration (i.e. "rising again") of the new – made possible by Christ's death, burial and resurrection, and applied to the believer's heart by the work of the Holy Spirit;
4. Baptism symbolizes and pictures the application of Christ's finished work by the Holy Spirit, who has "washed" believers from sin with pure water (cf. Mk 1:8; Titus 3:3-7; 1 Pet 3:21);[72] and

---

Jesus' death, and our identification with it, (4) Jesus' resurrection, and our identification with it, and (5) the coming resurrection for all believers (Henry G. Weston, "Baptism – A Symbol," in *The Madison Avenue Lectures* [reprint; Watertown: Roger Williams Heritage Archives, 1867], 133–134).

72. Baptists have been split on this last option. For example, Alvah Hovey saw baptism as symbolizing regeneration and washing away of sins, in addition to union with Christ's death, burial and resurrection (*Systematic,* 321-322). As we will see (below), the 1644 London Confession also advocates this position. So does Hiscox (*Principles and Practices,* 425). Also, see Weston's lecture, "Baptism – A Symbol," from the previous footnote.

In addition, William Kiffin held to this view. He believed believer's baptism had four purposes; (1) to show repentance, (2) to show a picture of regeneration, (3) to show being born of water and Spirit, and (4) "a symbol of our dying into sin, and living again to Christian newness of life," (William Kiffin, *Sober Discourse of Right to Church Communion - Wherein is proved by Scripture, the example of the Primitive times, and the practice of all that Have professed the Christian Religion: That no unbaptized person may Be regularly admitted to the Lord's Supper* [London, Printed by George Larkin, for Enoch Prosser, And the Rose and Crown in Sweethings - Alley, At the East End of the royal Exchange, 1681], ch. 2).

However, Kevin Bauder (and many modern Baptists) disagree with the purification from sins view (*Baptist Distinctives,* 39-44).

5. Baptism is a promise of a believer's future resurrection to glory with Father and Son.

How good are these arguments? The best thing to do is look at what the Scriptures say.

What the Word "Baptism" Means

This is a Greek word that has been imported into English. Its typical meaning to is immerse, plunge, dip or wash.[73] People figure out what words mean by seeing how they're used in everyday language. You don't need to rely on Greek dictionaries to know what "baptism" means; you can look at the Bible and see for yourself. In the following survey, we'll look at many uses of the word, both in the Greek Old Testament[74] and the New Testament, and see what we can find. Most of the uses don't give any contextual clues, but some do:

2 Kings 5:14

Naaman, the great Syrian commander, has leprosy. He sought help from Northern Kingdom of Israel. The prophet Elisha heard this news and seized the opportunity. He sent a messenger to tell Naaman, "Go! Wash seven times in the Jordan, and your flesh will return to you, and you will be clean," (2 Kgs 5:10, LXX). Of what does this "washing" consist?

The Scriptures tell us that, after some initial skepticism, Naaman did as he was told. "And so Naaman went down and **dipped** in the

---

73. See Walter Bauer, *A Greek English Lexicon of the New Testament and Other Early Christian Literature*, ed. Frederick W. Danker, 3rd ed. (Chicago: University of Chicago Press, 2000), BibleWorks. v.10., s.v. "1400 βαπτίζω."

74. Unless otherwise noted, all quotations from the Septuagint in this section are from Rick Brannan et al., eds., *The Lexham English Septuagint* (Bellingham, WA: Lexham Press, 2012).

Jordan seven times according to the word of Elisha ..." (2 Kgs 5:14, LXX). This word translated "dipped" is the Greek word "baptized."

Naaman washed himself. He dipped himself into the Jordan River seven times. He did not sprinkle water on his head. He did not simply pour water onto himself. He *dipped* himself. Elisha told him to wash, and he did just that. The nature of this "washing" strongly suggests an immersion; he plunged himself in (and, perhaps, under) the water seven times.

Judith 12:7

Likewise, the same word in the apocryphal book of Judith refers to a woman **bathing** or **washing** at a spring inside an armed camp (Judith 12:7). One Presbyterian scholar, J. Oliver Buswell, Jr., remarked about the Judith reference that "[s]urely this cannot mean that she was immersed."[75] He's right! Like all words, the one we usually translate as "baptize" has a range of meanings, depending on the context. As Buswell stated, "[i]f immersion is coupled with the act of baptism, the fact has to be learned from the context."[76]

Isaiah 21:4

This is a passage about the fall of the Babylonian Empire. Isaiah was looking far into the future. The Babylonians hadn't even conquered the Southern Kingdom of Judah, and yet Isaiah gives a prophesy which looks far beyond Babylon to the Medo-Persian Empire which would arise afterward.

Because we're looking at how the Scriptures use the Greek word βαπτίζω, we're looking at examples from the Greek translation of the

---

75. J. Oliver Buswell, Jr., *A Systematic Theology of the Christian Religion*, 2 vols. (Grand Rapids: Zondervan, 1962), 2:245.

76. Ibid.

Old Testament, which is sometimes a *bit* different than the Hebrew Old Testament. But, concentrate on what the word means. Here, look at what how Isaiah expresses his feelings in the Greek Old Testament rendering of Isaiah 21:3-4:

> *Because of this, my loins have been filled with faintness, and pangs have taken me like the woman giving birth; I did wrong by not hearing; I was hasty by not seeing. My heart goes astray, and lawlessness* **immerses** *me; my life stands in fear.*

It's clear Isaiah is terrified. He feels faint. He experiences sharp pains of anxiety, almost like those of a woman in labor! He even acknowledges his own responsibility; he didn't hear and didn't see what was coming. His heart has wandered, and he feels *immersed* or *baptized* in lawlessness. Think of the imagery; sprinkling or pouring doesn't work. In a colloquial way, Isaiah is saying he's *drowning* in lawlessness.

Matthew 3:16

This is the account of Jesus' baptism. We read, "[a]nd when Jesus was baptized, immediately he **went up from the water** and behold, the heavens were opened to him, and he saw the Spirit of God descending ... (Mt 3:16). It's tempting to read a lot into this statement. What does it mean that Jesus "went up from the water," and what does it tell us about the nature of the baptism? It could mean two things:

1. Immediately, as soon as Jesus rose up out of the water from being immersed, the heavens were torn open and the Spirit descended, or
2. Immediately, as soon as Jesus began to walk out of the river towards the bank, the heavens were torn open (etc., etc.).

The context doesn't answer it for us. Luke don't help, either (Lk 3:21), either. We'll have to interpret the usage here in light of clearer uses of the word.

Mark 7:3-4[77]

This is a passage where Jesus attacks the externalism and man-made ceremonial laws common in his day. The excerpt, below, is an explanatory aside from Mark:

> *For the Pharisees and all the Jews do not eat unless they **wash** their hands properly, holding to the tradition of the elders, and when they come from the marketplace, they do not eat unless they **wash**. And there are many other traditions that they observe, such as the **washing** of cups and pots and copper vessels and dining couches (Mk 7:3-4).*

The ceremonial washing of the hands was done by pouring; Jewish literature from around 200 A.D. makes this clear. The second reference is probably also about ceremonial hand washing, and indicates pouring or partial immersion. However, the ceremonial washing of various dishes is certainly by immersion; there are *extensive* and tedious Jewish writings which speak of the rules for using "immersion pools" for this very purpose.[78] There are even precise instructions about disassembling beds to immerse them, if they've been ceremonially defiled.[79]

---

77. See also Luke 11:38.

78. See the tractate Mikwaoth ("Immersion-pools"), in *Mishnah*, translated by Herbert Danby (New York: Oxford University Press, 1933).

79. See tractate Kelim ("Vessels") 19.1-6, in *Mishnah*.

John 3:23

The Apostle John tells us John the Baptist "was baptizing at Aenon near Salim, because water was plentiful there, and people were coming and being baptized," (Jn 3:23). Why did the water need to be "plentiful?" You don't need a lot of water to sprinkle or pour! You *do* need plenty of water if you immerse. This isn't definitive, but it suggests John baptized by immersion.

Acts 8:36-39

In the account of the Ethiopian eunuch who is evangelized by Philip, we read "as they were going along the road they came to some water, and the eunuch said, 'See, here is water! What prevents me from being baptized?' And he commanded the chariot to stop, and they both went **down into the water**, Philip and the eunuch, and he baptized him. And when they **came up out of the water**, the Spirit of the Lord carried Philip away …"

The word means what it says; you can't appeal to Greek and suggest it *really* means something else. In order to be baptized, both of them went *down into* the water. After the baptism, they "rose up from the water" (ἀνέβησαν ἐκ τοῦ ὕδατος). Buswell, a Presbyterian, disagrees. He suggests this means Philip and the Ethiopian man stepped into a puddle of water, Philip poured a bit of water on the man's head, then they exited the puddle.[80] This is desperate reasoning. This passage strongly suggests Philip baptized by immersion.

1 Corinthians 10:2

---

80. Buswell (*Systematic Theology*, 2:248).

The Apostle Paul is explaining how important it is to practice discipline in your personal life (1 Cor 9:24-27). That's why Christians today should learn from the example of the Israelites who came before them (1 Cor 10:6). In the same way that Christians have been immersed by the Holy Spirit and brought into union with Christ, "our fathers were all under the cloud, and all passed through the sea, and all were **baptized into Moses** in the cloud and in the sea ..." (1 Cor 10:1-2).

Paul isn't talking about the ordinance of baptism, of course. But, what does he mean by the use of the word? The sense is that the Israelites who escaped Egypt were baptized into union with Moses by two different means; the waters of the Red Sea and the cloud that led the way to Sinai.[81] That is, there was a *union and identity* between the people and their appointed leader, Moses.

What concept communicates this best – immersion or sprinkling? Because the means of this baptism are (1) the walls of water in the Red Sea, and (2) the cloud that led them to Sinai, the idea of a figurative immersion that unites them to Moses seems to fit better. The word likely means *immersion,* in this context.

Conclusion about the Word "Baptism"

Our survey of this word's usage in the Greek Old Testament and the New Testament shows it often means to *immerse* or *dip* (2 Kgs 5:14; Isa 21:4; Mk 7:3-4; Jn 3:23; Acts 8:36-39; 1 Cor 10:2), but it also has a more generic meaning of *washing* (Judith 12:7; Mk 7:3-4).

The Holy Spirit, Baptism and Washing Metaphors

---

81. I take the preposition ἐν to be describing the means by which the baptism happens. Most English Bible versions translate this in a spatial sense ("in the cloud"), in a wooden fashion.

The Scriptures use water metaphors about the Holy Spirit's work to describe the "baptism of the Spirit" in a New Covenant context. The Old Testament describes this future promise in several passages. In other areas, the Scriptures refer to divine forgiveness and pardon with *washing* metaphors, picturing the work of the Spirit in a believer's life.

Of course, these references aren't precisely the same as the *ordinance* of baptism itself. But, the point is that the Spirit's work both in Old and New Covenant members is pictured by metaphors of washing and cleansing. And, as we've seen, the *ordinance* of baptism is a picture of this inward spiritual reality, and the object lesson of believer's baptism ought to match the inward reality it shows and tells to the world. So, it'll be helpful to look at these metaphors and see what light they shed on the subject.

Old Testament Evidence

It's a tall order to summarize the Old Testament allusions to both the baptism of the Spirit, and the idea of moral purification through a divine "washing." Any Christian who reads her Old Testament can't escape these references. Here, I'll survey some of the more obvious passages and their implications for the concept of believer's baptism.

After his sin with Bathsheba, David prayed to God, "**wash me** thoroughly from my iniquity, and **cleanse me** from my sin!" (Ps 51:2). He continued, "**purge me** with hyssop, and I shall be **clean**; **wash me**, and I shall be whiter than snow," (Ps 51:7). This is a metaphor; David is asking God to cleanse him from his sin. To be sure, David is already a believer. But, the point is that divine forgiveness is a moral cleansing of the soul.

Likewise, Solomon wrote, "there are those who are **clean** in their own eyes, but are not **washed** of their filth," (Prov 30:12). There have always been hypocrites who think they're morally pure, cleansed from all unrighteousness and "square" with God. They're wrong. They're actually morally polluted, in a figurative sense. The concept is a moral uncleanness *as a status* ("you're a criminal before God"), which results in ceremonial uncleanness ("therefore, you're unfit to approach God").

God, through the prophet Isaiah, pleaded with the Israelites to **"wash yourselves; make yourselves clean;** remove the evil of your deeds from before my eyes," (Isa 1:16). They're morally unclean because of their sinfulness, so God can't and won't look at them. He doesn't want their sacrifices or prayers – they're all pretense, anyway.

What can they do? God explains, "cease to do evil, learn to do good; seek justice, correct oppression; bring justice to the fatherless, plead the widow's cause," (Isa 1:17). The answer is to return to covenant faithfulness. Believers ought to act like it, so start now! Loving obedience brings moral cleansing and purification. No amount of outward conformity can cleanse a heart and mind that's far from God (Jer 2:22). Instead, God demands a moral reformation that will wash them clean, purifying them from all unrighteousness:

*O Jerusalem, **wash your heart from evil**,*
that you may be saved.
How long shall your wicked thoughts
lodge within you? (Jer 4:14)

In Isaiah 32:15, the prophet Isaiah warns the complacent women of Judah that judgment is coming. The land will be desolate, destruction will reign, wild animals will roam the abandoned cities. This will continue "until the Spirit is **poured upon us** from on high, and the wilderness becomes a fruitful field, and the fruitful field is deemed a forest," (Isa 32:15). The imagery is that God will pour out the Spirit onto the people and the land, when the New and better covenant arrives. Of course, we shouldn't imagine God with a pitcher pouring out the Spirit from on high. But, the imagery here is clearly pouring, not immersion.

In the same way, God promises the Israelities, "I will **pour water on the thirsty land, and streams on the dry ground; I will pour my Spirit upon your offspring**, and my blessing on your descendants," (Isa 44:3). Again, the metaphor is *pouring*. Ezekiel relayed God's message that, "I will not hide my face anymore from them, when I **pour out my Spirit** upon the house of Israel, declares the Lord God," (Ezek 39:29). God also moved Joel to write, "I will **pour out** my Spirit on all flesh ..." (Joel 2:28).

The Scriptures also use the imagery of sprinkling to refer to the New Covenant. This refers to the sacrificial system of atonement, where blood was sprinkled on the altar to atone for sins (Lev 1:5; 5:9, 16, etc.). Ezekiel explained, "I will **sprinkle clean water on you**, and you shall be **clean** from all your uncleannesses, and from all your idols I will **cleanse** you," (Ezek 36:25). Isaiah promised that the suffering Messiah would "**sprinkle** many nations," (Isa 52:15).

Old Testament Analysis

In summary, when the Old Testament describes how the Spirit will come, His work is described as *pouring;* a vivid metaphor that pictures the Spirit showering over you and drenching you. The ideal experience of a covenant member, and God's command to disobedient members of His covenant family, is to be *cleansed* or *washed* from unrighteousness. This could refer to both salvation (the initial, objective cleansing of the soul) or ongoing growth or discipline as a believer. Regardless, moral purification is repeatedly expressed as a divine *washing* or *cleansing*, often through *pouring*. This, too, is a work of the Spirit.

Baptism is an object lesson and parable of an inward, spiritual reality. Your sins have been washed away and you've been united with Christ. More specifically, *the Spirit* has done this to you. The figures of *washing, cleansing,* and *pouring* are each complementary ways of expressing one objective reality – the spiritual birth.

The references to *sprinkling* refer to atonement and have more of a priestly meaning; the Book of Hebrews brings this out in the New Testament (see discussion, below). The Spirit is the agent who cleanses you by applying Christ's atoning blood to your soul, in a figurative way.

New Testament Evidence

John the Baptist promised "I have baptized you with water, but he will baptize you with the Holy Spirit," (Mk 1:8; cf. Mt 3:11; Jn 1:26-27). He's referring to the baptism of the Spirit, which the Old Testament passages depicted as pouring or sprinkling. Jesus promised the disciples would be "**clothed** with power from on high," (Lk 24:49), and ordered them to wait for the baptism John promised (Acts 1:5, 8).

When it did come, Luke described this baptism as a **filling** of the Spirit (Acts 2:4) that Jesus **poured out** from on high (Acts 2:33). It's very interesting that Luke records Peter using the same terminology of *pouring* that Isaiah and Joel used. Later, Luke tells us that the Spirit **fell** on Cornelius and the others who believed (Acts 10:44; see also Acts 8:16), just like He had at Pentecost (Acts 11:15). Because the Spirit is often described with water metaphors, you almost get the impression God threw a bucket of water onto Cornelius and his household from on high, drenching them! Luke went on to clarify the Spirit had been **poured out** onto them (Acts 10:46).

Paul, when he recounted his salvation experience, explained that Ananias urged him, "and now why do you wait? Rise and be baptized and **wash away your sins**, calling on his name," (Acts 22:16). If Paul calls on Jesus' name, then his sin will be washed away. The baptism pictures this spiritual reality.

This is what Jesus alluded to when He told Nicodemus "unless one is **born of water and the Spirit**, he cannot enter the kingdom of God," (Jn 3:5). Water and Spirit are synonymous; the former paints a picture of the latter's work. You can't enter God's kingdom unless the Spirit washes your sins away *first*. Jesus referred to this supernatural "washing" when He told the disciples, at the Last Supper, " And you are **clean**, but not every one of you," (Jn 13:10). Clean how? In a moral sense, and Judas was the "unclean one" in the group.

Likewise, Paul explains elsewhere that something objective has happened to believers that changed their status before God. "But you were **washed**, you were sanctified, you were justified in the name of the Lord Jesus Christ and by the Spirit of our God," (1 Cor 6:11). This inward washing is synonymous with being "made holy" (sanctified) and declared righteous (justified). How was this accomplished? By the Spirit, who washed them clean and changed their standing before the Lord!

This is what's happened to all believers, as a corporate group. Paul mentioned that Christ **"cleansed her** *[i.e. the entire church]* by the washing of water by the word," (Eph 5:26, RSV).[82]

In a similar way, Paul explained to Titus:

> *But when the goodness and loving kindness of God our Savior appeared, he saved us, not because of works done by us in righteousness, but according to his own mercy,* **by the washing of regeneration and renewal of the Holy Spirit**, *whom he* **poured out** *on us richly through Jesus Christ our Savior, so that being justified by his grace we might become heirs according to the hope of eternal life (Titus 3:4-7).*

God saves people, but how? He does it "by the washing and regeneration of the Holy Spirit," (Titus 3:5). The divine cleansing brings

---

82. Some English translations render the last bit "**with** the word." The best sense seems to be to understand the "word" (i.e. the Scriptures) to be the means by which the Spirit cleanses unbelievers and makes them Christians. After all, in the Apostle Paul's famous "armor of God" illustration, the sword of the Spirit is the word of God (Ephesians 6).

spiritual life, and the Father pours the Spirit out upon new believers through Jesus.

The writer to the Hebrews stated that Christ's once for all sacrifice is infinitely better than any of the Old Covenant parables. His blood sacrifice will "**purify our conscience** from dead works to serve the living God," (Heb 9:14). Again, we have the concepts of cleansing and purification. His atoning blood **makes purification** for sins (Heb 1:3); it makes people holy.

The first covenant was inaugurated by the blood of animal sacrifices, which Moses **sprinkled** upon the altar (Ex 24:1-8). The blood of the animal sacrifices purified people from their sins (Heb 9:22). In the same way:

> *Thus it was necessary for the copies of the heavenly things to be **purified with these rites**, but the heavenly things themselves with better sacrifices than these. For Christ has entered, not into holy places made with hands, which are copies of the true things, but into heaven itself, now to appear in the presence of God on our behalf.*
>
> *Nor was it to offer himself repeatedly, as the high priest enters the holy places every year with blood not his own, for then he would have had to suffer repeatedly since the foundation of the world. But as it is, he has appeared once for all at the end of the ages to put away sin by the sacrifice of himself (Heb 9:23-26).*

In the same way as Moses inaugurated the Old Covenant by sprinkling the blood of the animal sacrifices, so Christ has inaugurated the New Covenant by the sprinkling of His own blood on the figurative altar in heaven, above. The difference is that the Old Covenant sacrifices didn't convey a permanent **cleansing** (Heb 10:2), "for it is impossible for the blood of bulls and goats to take away sins" in an enduring sense (Heb 10:4). But now, in the New Covenant, "we have been **sanctified** through the offering of the body of Jesus Christ once for all," (Heb 10:10). Believers have been **cleansed**, purified and made holy once for all in a definitive, permanent way.

This is why the writer urged Jewish Christians to not shrink back and be anonymous Christians in the synagogues. Instead, "let us draw near with a true heart in full assurance of faith, with **our hearts sprinkled clean** from an evil conscience and our **bodies washed with pure water**," (Heb 10:22). Christ's atonement has been sprinkled on the figurative altar of our hearts, applied by Christ the High Priest, working through the Spirit. His atoning blood sanctifies His people (Heb 13:12) "by the blood of the eternal covenant" (Heb 13:20), which is applied by the Spirit in all those pouring and sprinkling metaphors from the Old Testament.

James uses the "cleansing as moral and spiritual renewal" metaphor, just like David did. He urged actions, not words. "Draw near to God, and he will draw near to you. **Cleanse your hands**, you sinners, and **purify your hearts**, you double-minded," (Jas 4:8).

The Apostle Peter explained that Christians were chosen for salvation according to the Father's foreknowledge, for the purpose of sanctification of the Holy Spirit and "for obedience to Jesus Christ and **for sprinkling with his blood**," (1 Pet 1:2). The figure of Noah and his family being saved through the floodwaters is analogous to the baptism of the Spirit. "Baptism, which corresponds to this, now saves you …" (1 Pet 3:20-21).

New Testament Analysis

The various descriptions of the Spirit *clothing, falling upon, being poured out onto* or *filling* new believers are indisputable. At first glance, none of these analogies seem to come close to implying *immersion.* However, consider the imagery these terms are meant to convey:

- *Clothing*: You almost picture yourself wrapped in a cloak or a blanket, enveloped by the Spirit.
- *Falling upon*: Again, one gets the idea of being drenched by the Spirit from on high by a sudden deluge.
- *Poured out*: Given the other metaphors of *clothing* and *falling upon*, this should be interpreted as a torrent or flood unleased upon the believer, not a dainty pour from a dixie cup.
- *Filling*: This corresponds well with the other metaphors; you certainly have *a lot* of the Spirit if He figuratively fills the believer with His power and presence!

These metaphors convey a startling imagery of the Spirit's work in regeneration. This work is called *baptism.* But, remember, "baptism" is a Greek word. It has no meaning at all in English, in and of itself. So, the question is this - which use of the word best carries the freight of all this imagery? Which method of "baptizing" best captures this imagery of *clothing, filling, falling upon* and *pouring*?

Immersion seems best. Unless one is prepared to literally *drench and soak* a baptismal candidate, a few modest sprinkles or a polite pour just won't do.

However, what of the allusions to divine cleansing and purification by the *sprinkling* of the Spirit? The answer is that these references are more about *divine application of the atonement* by the Spirit on the figurative "altar of your soul." In other words, the "cleansing" and "washing" metaphors speak to the Spirit's work and are applicable to the baptism discussion. The "sprinkling" passages are about Christ's work of blood atonement and are captured in the object lessons of the Lord's Supper. They are not applicable to the baptism question.[83]

---

83. To be sure, Ezekiel uses sprinkling to refer to the New Covenant (Ezek 36:25). But is he referring to regeneration by the baptism of the Spirit? Or, is he referring to a definitive atonement and cleansing from sins? Ezekiel says it's the latter; "I will sprinkle clean water on you, and you shall be clean from fall your uncleannesses, and from all your idols I will cleanse you," (Ezek 36:25). When John the Baptist refers to

In the end, the weight of Romans 6 (discussed earlier, above) and the "buried in baptism" references cannot be overcome. As Adoniram Judson has remarked:[84]

> [W]e may rest assured, that if baptism had consisted in sprinkling or pouring, or any partial application of water whatever, though we might possibly have heard of being <u>washed in baptism</u>, we should never have heard of being <u>buried in baptism</u>; for there being no resemblance, between such application of water and a burial, there could have been no propriety in representing baptism under such a figure.
>
> But there is a confessed resemblance between immersion and a burial; and since the phrase, buried in baptism, is sanctioned by the highest authority, even divine inspiration, we have invincible proof, that baptism consists not in sprinkling or pouring, but in immersion.

Believer's baptism pictures the sinner's union with Christ in His death, burial and resurrection. It also pictures the washing away of sins; the filling and clothing of the sinner with the Spirit, Who has fallen upon the lost sinner and made him be born again of water and Spirit. It's a living object lesson on an objective, inward reality. Just as

---

the baptism of the Spirit, one's mind *does* tend to wander to passages like Ezekiel 36:25. But, the passages in Acts that describe this promised baptism use metaphors like *filling, pouring* or *falling upon*.

It does seem somewhat forced to draw a sharp distinction between (1) the application of the atonement by the Spirit in the sprinkling of Christ's blood, and (2) the result of the sprinkling, which is the new birth of regeneration; a spiritual reality pictured by the cleansing and washing metaphors of believer's baptism. But, they *are* different. The Sprit applies Christ's work, then fills, immerses and clothes the believer. He's poured out and deluged upon the new Christian. Logically, there is a sequence, even if its difficult to imagine experientially.

84. Judson (*Christian Baptism*, 16-17).

the Israelites were baptized into Moses by the waters of the Red Sea, so Christians are baptized into Christ by the figurative, cleansing waters of the Spirit, Who cleanses us from all unrighteousness.

The 1644 London Confession sums up the Baptist position best. William Lumpkin wrote, "[p]erhaps no Confession of Faith has had so formative an influence on Baptist life as this one." It reads this about believer's baptism:[85]

> *The way and manner of the dispensing of this Ordinance the Scripture holds out to be dipping or plunging the whole body under the water: it being a signe, must answer the thing signified, which are these: **first**, the washing of the whole soule in the bloud of Christ; **Secondly**, that interest the Saints have in the death, burial, and resurrection; **thirdly**, together with a confirmation of our faith, that as certainly as the body is buried under water, and riseth againe, so certainly shall the bodies of the Saints be raised by the power of Christ, in the day of the resurrection, to reigne with Christ.*

More could be said. These are the key points:

1. The New Covenant scriptures are the only place where New Covenant members learn how to worship Yahweh in a New Covenant context;

---

85. Lumpkin, "London Confession (1644)," in *Baptist Confessions,* Article 40. See (also from Lumpkin) the Somerset Confession (1656), Article 24.

   Interestingly, Thomas Helwys' "A Short Confession (1610)" doesn't mention the figure of death to self and resurrection to new life *at all*. It only focuses on the symbolism of purification and washing by the Spirit. It "witnesseth and signifieth, the Lord Jesus doth inwardly baptize the repentant, faithful man, in the laver of regeneration and renewing of the Holy Ghost, washing the soul from all pollution and sin, by the virtue and merit of His bloodshed; and by the power and working of the Holy Ghost, the true, heavenly, spiritual, living Water, cleanseth the inward evil of the soul, and maketh it heavenly, spiritual, and living, in true righteousness or goodness," (Lumpkin, "A Short Confession [1610]," Article 30, in *Baptist Confessions,* 110).

2. New Covenant membership (believers alone) is *completely different* from Old Covenant membership (mixed multitude);
3. Regeneration is the New Covenant sign, which has replaced external circumcision;
4. Believer's baptism is the external sign which signifies, shows and tells the world that the person has been saved by God's grace;
5. Immersion is the only figure which captures the full significance of Christ's death, burial and resurrection and, thus, shows forth the blessings of the New Covenant in (a) the believer's washing from sin by the Spirit, (b) the death of the person and resurrection to new life in Christ, and (c) his future resurrection to glory as a member of Christ's coming kingdom

It is clear Baptists have a very different view of the ordinance than many of our Christian brothers and sisters. This strikes right at the heart of what the New Covenant is, what a New Covenant member is, what the ordinance of baptism means, and who it's intended for. These aren't trivial issues; they're vital.

6: BAPTISTS ON THE LORD'S SUPPER

> **SYNOPSIS:**
>
> 1. The Lord's Supper is only for Christians who are, by definition, members of the New Covenant.
> 2. There are many ideas about what the Lord's Supper means. The Scriptures teach the Supper is a memorial about Christ's death on the cross for sinners, to inaugurate the New Covenant, and His promise to return one day for His people. The bread and the cup are object lessons to help Christians remember these precious truths, and the Supper is a vehicle for the Spirit to re-apply the truths they represent to the believer's heart and mind.
> 3. Believer's baptism and church membership *are not* prerequisites to partake of the Lord's Supper. However, every Christian has a divine responsibility to be obedient to believer's baptism and to formally join herself to a local congregation.
> 4. There are several things a local congregation can do about the Lord's Supper, in light of these principles.

The ordinance of the Lord's Supper has generated a lot of discussion over the years. People have written a lot about it, and not all of it is worth reading. The 1833 *New Hampshire Confession of Faith* summarizes it nicely when it reads that it's an ordinance "in which the members of the Church, by the sacred use of bread and wine, are to commemorate together the dying love of Christ; preceded always by solemn self-examination," (Article 14).[86] It's clear the Confession understands that *only Christians* can celebrate this ordinance.

---

86. Cited from Lumpkin, *Baptist Confessions,* 366.

The 1689 *London Baptist Confession of Faith* also explains the Lord's Supper is only for believers:[87]

> *The supper of the Lord Jesus was instituted by him the same night wherein he was betrayed, to be observed in his churches, unto the end of the world, for the perpetual remembrance, and shewing forth the sacrifice of himself in his death, confirmation of the faith of believers in all the benefits thereof, their spiritual nourishment, and growth in him, their further engagement in, and to all duties which they owe to him; and to be a bond and pledge of their communion with him, and with each other (30.1)*

> *All ignorant and ungodly persons, as they are unfit to enjoy communion with Christ, so are they unworthy of the Lord's table, and cannot, without great sin against him, while they remain such, partake of these holy mysteries, or be admitted thereunto; yea, whosoever shall receive unworthily, are guilty of the body and blood of the Lord, eating and drinking judgment to themselves (30.8).*

Likewise, the more modern GARBC *Articles of Faith* (2014) contains the same language:[88]

> *We believe that the Lord's Supper is the commemoration of His death until He come, and should be preceded always by solemn self-examination. We believe that the Biblical order of the ordinances is baptism first and then the Lord's Supper, and that participants in the Lord's Supper should be immersed*

---

87. Retrieved from https://reformed.org/documents/index.html.

88. Retrieved from https://www.garbc.org/about-us/beliefs-constitution/articles-of-faith/.

believers.

Who is the Lord's Supper For?

Here, we'll look at two passages about the Lord's Supper, and consider what the Bible says about who it's for, what it means, and who can partake.

The Gospels

Matthew 26:26-29	Mark 14:22-25	Luke 22:17-20
		17 And he took a cup, and when he had given thanks he said, "Take this, and divide it among yourselves;
		18 for I tell you that from now on I shall not drink of the fruit of the vine until the kingdom of God comes."
26 Now as they were eating, Jesus took bread, and blessed, and broke it, and gave it to the disciples and said, "Take, eat; this is my body."	22 And as they were eating, he took bread, and blessed, and broke it, and gave it to them, and said, "Take; this is my body."	19 And he took bread, and when he had given thanks he broke it and gave it to them, saying, "This is my body which is given for you. Do this in remembrance of me."
27 And he took a cup, and when he had given thanks he gave it to them, saying, "Drink of it, all of you;	23 And he took a cup, and when he had given thanks he gave it to them, and they all drank of it.	20 And likewise the cup after supper, saying, "This cup which is poured out for you is the new covenant in my blood.
28 for this is my blood of the covenant, which is poured out for many for the forgiveness of sins.	24 And he said to them, "This is my blood of the covenant, which is poured out for many.	
29 I tell you I shall not drink again of this fruit of the vine until that day when I drink it new with you in my Father's kingdom."	25 Truly, I say to you, I shall not drink again of the fruit of the vine until that day when I drink it new in the kingdom of God."	

These passages teach the same thing, and they show the Lord's Supper is for Christians only. The bread represents Jesus' body; "this is my body," (Mk 14:22). Jesus told the disciples His body "is given for you," (Lk 22:19). The ordinance is for people who have repented and believed in what Jesus gave His body for.

The Apostle Peter wrote, "Because even Christ suffered for sins once for all, a righteous man for unrighteous people, in order to bring you [believers] to God; although He was put to death in the body, He was given life by the Spirit," (1 Pet 3:18).[89] Jesus told His disciples to "take [and] eat" this bread (Mt 26:26), and Christians would later understand the object lessons inherent in these simple symbols.

After the dinner (Lk 22:20), Jesus commanded all the disciples to drink the wine. What is the wine's significance? Jesus told them, "this cup which is poured out for you is the new covenant in my blood," (Lk 22:20). The wine, red in color, represented Jesus blood which would be shed the next morning. He's the perfect sacrifice who atoned for sins "once for all" (1 Pet 3:18). The Old and obsolete covenant would be replaced by a New and better covenant, enacted on better promises (Heb 8:6-18). The writer of the letter to the Hebrew explained,

> But as it is, he has appeared once for all at the end of the age to put away sin by the sacrifice of himself. And just as it is appointed for men to die once, and after that comes judgment, so Christ, having been offered once to bear the sins of many, will appear a second time, not to deal with sin but to save those who are eagerly waiting for him (Heb 9:26-28)

And,

---

89. This is my own translation.

> But when Christ had offered for all time a single sacrifice for sins, he sat down at the right hand of God, then to wait until his enemies should be made a stool for his feet. For by a single offering he has perfected for all time those who are sanctified. And the Holy Spirit also bears witness to us; for after saying,
>
> > 'This is the covenant that I will make with them after those days, says the Lord: I will put my laws on their hearts, and write them on their minds,'
>
> then he adds,
>
> > 'I will remember their sins and their misdeeds no more.'
>
> Where there is forgiveness of these, there is no longer any offering for sin (Heb 10:12-18).

Who is the New Covenant for? We've already seen that the prophesy from Jeremiah says the New Covenant is only for believers. And, at the Last Supper, Jesus makes this clear. He shed His blood to inaugurate the New Covenant, which is "poured out for many for the forgiveness of sins," (Mt 26:28), "poured out for many," (Mk 14:24) and "poured out for you," (Lk 20:20).

The New Covenant is for believers alone, and Jesus understood that. He even gave them instructions to eat the bread and drink the wine "in remembrance of me," (Lk 20:19; see the remark "likewise" in Lk 20:20 for the wine). People who don't love Jesus and don't belong to Him by repentance from sins and faith in His finished work can't observe the ordinance the way Jesus commanded, because His broken body and shed blood mean *nothing* to them. They aren't part of the New Covenant family.

1 Corinthians 11

The Apostle Paul quoted the Gospel account when he rebuked the church at Corinth. Paul explained that Jesus' body was broken for believers, and they should celebrate the ordinance "in remembrance" of Jesus (1 Cor 11:23-24). They should also drink the wine from the cup as another object lesson, a reminder that Jesus' blood "is the new covenant in my blood," (1 Cor 11:25). Every time they drink the wine at the Lord's Supper ("as often as you drink it," 1 Cor 11:25), they must do so "in remembrance of me," (1 Cor 11:25). Why should they do this? Paul explains:

> *For as often as you eat this bread and drink the cup, you proclaim the Lord's death until he comes (1 Cor 11:26).*

Paul tells us that, by observing the Lord's Supper, Christians do three things:

1. They proclaim Christ's death (and the Gospel which accompanies it) to the world,
2. They remember His death as a solemn memorial, through the symbols of the bread and wine, to be used for serious self-reflection
3. and they remember His precious promise to return one day, to judge the living and the dead and set all things right

The key thing to remember is that *this is for Christians*, not unbelievers. It's for New Covenant members. There is no hint *anywhere* in the New Testament that the Lord's Supper is for unbelievers.

Is Christ "in" the Lord's Supper?

After surveying the biblical data (above), this isn't really a difficult question to answer. But, it's *become* difficult because of the mass of tradition the ordinance carries with it. There are four basic positions:[90]

1. The bread and wine literally *are* the body and blood of Christ
2. The bread and wine *contain* the body and blood of Christ
3. The bread and wine *spiritually contain* the body and blood of Christ
4. The bread and wine *represent* the body and blood of Christ

It's clear the Bible teaches the fourth view, but we'll very briefly discuss the different options.

The Roman Catholic View

The first is the traditional Roman Catholic position, and it cannot be defended from scripture. We know this, because we've just surveyed the relevant passages and they don't teach this. The Roman Catholic Church teaches that, through the sacerdotal formula of the rightly ordained priest, the ordinary bread and wine *literally become* Christ's body and blood (i.e. the doctrine of transubstantiation).[91] This doctrine was codified at the Fourth Lateran Council, in 1215.[92]

And, the congregation participates in a literal re-sacrifice of Christ's body and blood as they observe communion.[93] In a very real

---

90. Erickson (*Christian Theology*, 1121).

91. On the development of the doctrine of transubstantiation in history, see Beale (*Historical Theology*, 1:506 – 513).

92. See Canon 1 from the Fourth Lateran Council, in *Decrees of the Ecumenical Councils*, ed. Norman J. Tanner S.J., 2 vols. (Washington D.C., Georgetown University Press, 1990), 1:230.

93. "The Eucharist is thus a sacrifice because it *re-presents* (makes present) the sacrifice of the cross ..." (*Catechism of the Catholic Church* [New York: Doubleday, 1995], Article 1366).

sense, the Lord's Supper is necessary for salvation, because the Roman Catholic Church has no concept of final justification in this life. In fact, Roman Catholic doctrine damns everyone to hell who disagrees with its position:[94]

> **If any one saith, that the sacraments of the New Law are not necessary unto salvation**, *but superfluous; and that, without them, or without the desire thereof, men obtain of God, through faith alone, the grace of justification;—though all [the sacraments] are not indeed necessary for every individual:* **let him be anathema**.

Scripture does not support any of this; it doesn't even hint at it. This is an abominable perversion of a beautiful ordinance.

The Lutheran View

Martin Luther taught that the Lord's Supper was[95]

> *… the true body and blood of our Lord Jesus Christ, under the bread and wine, given unto us Christians to eat and to drink, as it was instituted by Christ himself.*

One key distinction is that Lutherans do not believe that, by way of a formula repeated by a sacerdotal priest, the bread and wine *turn into* Christ's bread and body. Instead, when Christians celebrate the

---

94. Philip Schaff (ed.), "The Council of Trent, Seventh Session, Canon 4," in *The Creeds of Christendom*, 3 vols. (New York: Harper & Brothers, 1890), 2:120. I suggest every Protestant read the Council of Trent, Seventh Session, Canons 1 – 13 for more on the Lord's Supper and the blasphemy of the Roman Catholic position.

95. Philip Schaff (ed.), *Luther's Small Catechism*, Part 5, in *The Creeds of Christendom*, 3 vols. (New York: Harper & Brothers, 1890), 3:90.

Lord's Supper, Christ becomes present "in and under the bread and wine."[96]

In addition, the Lutherans do not believe the ordinance saves anybody, else men would be justified by the Mass, and not by faith! The Augsburg Confession (1530) explains, "therefore the Mass has been instituted that faith in them which use the Sacrament may remember what benefits it receiveth by Christ, and that it may raise and comfort the fearful conscience."[97] Indeed, the Lutherans wrote that "no sane person" could ever believe the Mass actually saved anybody.[98]

In the year 1529, the Swiss Reformer Ulrich Zwingli met with the German Reformer Martin Luther at Marburg Castle, in modern day Germany. They sought to bring about a union of the Swiss and German reform movements, but they famously clashed over whether Christ was actually present in the bread and wine of the Lord's Supper. Luther, as we've seen, believed He *was* present and pointed to Christ's words, "Take; this **is** my body," (Mk 14:22).

Zwingli protested that Christ was being figurative, but Luther would have none of it. He wrote, "mark this and remember it well. For upon these words rest our whole argument ..."[99] The two reform movements never reconciled, and the Reformed and Lutheran camps remain divided on this issue today.[100]

---

96. Theodore G. Tappert (ed.), "Luther's Large Catechism," in *The Book of Concord* (Philadelphia: Fortress, 1959), 447.

97. Philip Schaff (ed.), *The Augsburg Confession*, Second Part, in *The Creeds of Christendom*, 3 vols. (New York: Harper & Brothers, 1890), 3:38.

98. Tappert, "Apology of the Augsburg Confession," Article 15, in *Book of Concord*, 251.

99. Tappert ("Luther's Large Catechism," in *Book of Concord,* 448 – 449).

100. For a stirring account of the 1529 meeting at Marburg, see Phillip Schaff, *History of the Christian Church*, 8 vols. (New York: Charles Scribner's Sons, 1910), 7:620 - 650.

The Reformed View

The Reformed churches believe Christ is *spiritually* present in the Lord's Supper. To suggest that the bread and wine literally become Christ's body and blood, by way of an incantation by a priest, "is repugnant, not to Scripture alone, but even to common-sense and reason."[101] Instead, individuals who partake of the Supper receive tangible and real spiritual nourishment:[102]

> *Worthy receivers, outwardly partaking of the visible elements in this sacrament, do then also inwardly by faith, really and indeed, yet not carnally and corporally, but spiritually, receive and feed upon Christ crucified, and all benefits of his death: the body and blood of Christ being then not corporally or carnally in, with, or under the bread and wine, yet as really, but spiritually, present to the faith of believers in that ordinance, as the elements themselves are, to their outward senses*

Believers "feed upon the body and blood of Christ" in a spiritual sense; not in a literal way, "but in a spiritual manner; yet truly and really"[103] through the mediation of the Spirit.[104] The Spirit, one Reformed theologian concluded, "is the agent who unites us to Christ and therefore communicates Christ and his benefits to believers."[105]

---

101. Westminster Confession of Faith (29.6).

102. Westminster Confession of Faith (29.7).

103. Westminster Larger Catechism, Q 170. Retrieved from the Center for Reformed Theology and Apologetics, at https://reformed.org/documents/wlc_w_proofs/index.html.

104. Horton (*Systematic Theology*, 813).
105. Horton (*Systematic Theology*, 814).

The Memorial View

This is also called the "Zwinglian" position, because it agrees with the Swiss reformer Ulrich Zwingli. This is the view most Baptists take, and it's the view the scriptural evidence supports. Nowhere in the Gospels, or in 1 Corinthians 11, does the bible suggest the first two positions. Luther's position is the result of a stubborn literalism, colored by a lifetime of influence from the heretical Roman Catholic position. The Reformed view represents a *via media* between the Lutheran and Memorial views. Indeed, you can chart the evolution of the various views of the doctrine of the Lord's Supper in a continuum like this:

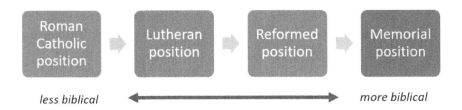

Jesus told the apostles to eat the bread and drink the wine in remembrance of Him (1 Cor 11:25; Lk 22:19). This shows the ordinance is a *memorial of remembrance* for His broken body and shed blood, which inaugurated the new covenant. The Apostle Paul's commentary is that, " for as often as you eat this bread and drink the cup, you proclaim the Lord's death until he comes," (1 Cor 11:26).

This shows the Lord's Supper is also a *public proclamation of Christ's imminent return*. At heart, the Lord's Supper is about renewal;[106] it's a vehicle Christ gave us to remember what He did, and to look forward to His return. More than that, it's a vehicle for the Spirit to apply the truth represented by the Supper to a Christian's

---

106. Hammett (*Biblical Foundations*, 281 – 282).

heart and mind. It helps us grow in Christ and remember what He did for His people.

Are Baptism and Church Membership Requirements to Observe the Lord's Supper?

No, they aren't. The Bible doesn't say a Christian has to be baptized, or a member of a local church in order to partake of the Lord's Supper. Instead, those two requirements are more about being an obedient Christian than anything else. No matter what you read by a well-meaning pastor or theologian, the fact remains that the New Testament *never* says a Christian must be baptized or a member of a local church in order to celebrate the ordinance.

The biblical evidence (above) supports three requirements:[107]

1. The person must be a Christian
2. The person must understand what the ordinance means
3. The person must be repentant after honest self-examination

But, first, two caveats:

1. Every Christian must be baptized

If you know you should be baptized, and you're deliberately refusing to be baptized, then you're in rebellion and you're committing a sin. If you haven't had an opportunity to be baptized,

---

107. This is also Erickson's conclusion (*Christian Theology,* 1132). Henry Thiessen agreed, and wrote, "[t]he conditions of participating in the Lord's Supper are regeneration and a life of obedience to Christ … Baptism should precede the Lord's Supper, but it is not a *condition* to participation in it. There is no precept to that effect, and there is no proof that believers were excluded from the Lord's Supper until they were baptized (Acts 2:47; 4:4; 5:14; 6:1, 7; 9:31, 35, 42; 11:24). Nor is church membership a condition. This is the 'table of the Lord" (1 Cor 10:21) and not the church's table," (*Introductory Lectures in Systematic Theology* [Grand Rapids: Eerdmans, 1949], 431).

you need to speak to your pastor as soon as possible.

2. Every Christian must join a local church

When a Christian joins a church, he's pledging to be in covenant with other believers in that specific congregation. He's saying he plans to worship the Lord, serve the brethren, and minister and witness to the lost with the people in that church. He's joining a community, and formally identifying with that community for encouragement, growth, and safety.

If you're know you ought to join a local church, and you're deliberately not doing so, then you're in rebellion and committing sin. I urge you to speak to your pastors about this as soon as possible.

The argument that the Lord's Supper is restricted to baptized church members is an inference, not an explicit teaching. The train of thought goes like this:[108]

1. The Lord's Supper is for Christians; people who are part of the New Covenant,
2. and, the Bible teaches that every Christian is supposed to be baptized,
3. and, the Bible teaches that every Christian is supposed to join

---

108. See, for example, Hammett (*Biblical Foundations,* 287). He wrote, "since believer's baptism is required for church membership, and the Lord's Supper is for the church, believer's baptism is required to celebrate the Lord's Supper in unity and communion with other Baptists. To do otherwise is to denigrate baptism."

I especially urge the reader to examine the sixth chapter of William Kiffin's work on this issue (*Sober Discourse,* ch 6). The chapter is a series of common, hypothetical objections to the idea that believer's baptism is a prerequisite to the Lord's Supper, followed by his answers as to why it *is* a prerequisite. Kiffin's answers show he assumes his conclusions and that his entire argument is built upon inferences, like a tottering house of cards.

Likewise, Larry Oats observed, "since the Lord's Supper is a local church ordinance, and since baptism is a requirement for church membership, only saved and baptized persons should participate in the Communion," ("GPA 614 – Baptist Polity").

a local church for encouragement, accountability and to serve the Lord,
4. and, the Lord's Supper is observed by churches which are *theoretically* full of baptized believers who are church members
5. and, after all, Paul wrote to the church at Corinth, which was full of baptized believers who were church members,
6. so, the Lord's Supper is for baptized believers who are church members!

This is a good train of thought, and every pastor should encourage believers to be baptized and join a local church. But, Jesus didn't say these were prerequisites to observing the Lord's Supper. Neither did Paul. Instead, the ordinance is just for believers who are part of the New Covenant. As I said before, believer's baptism and church membership are more about *obedience* than anything else.

But, before I offer my suggestion to pastors about how to handle this issue in a practical way, I need to admit this much – my position is not the normal Baptist position. Most Baptists believe baptism and church membership *are* prerequisites for observing the Lord's Supper. One Baptist theologian provided a classic list of reasons why. As we'll see, these reason have more to do with inferences and slippery slope arguments than Biblical commands.

Arguments for believer's baptism and church membership as prerequisites for the lord's supper

Augustus Strong was (and still is) a very influential Baptist theologian, who published the last revision of his systematic theology in 1906. In his text, he listed many reasons why believer's baptism and local church membership are prerequisites to observing the Lord's Supper. Many Baptists, particularly those in the fundamentalist-evangelical camp, still follow his arguments. For example, Rolland

McCune was a long-time professor of systematic theology at Detroit Baptist Theological Seminary. In his own work, he followed Strong's arguments and concluded that "open communion" (i.e. allowing any believer to partake, regardless of baptism and church membership status) "is highly inconsistent and unbiblical."[109]

Therefore, Strong's list is probably the best argument a Baptist can find. I've provided it below, along with some brief discussion. Unless I note otherwise, I've provided them exactly as he wrote them:[110]

The ordinance of baptism was instituted and administered long before the Supper.

This objection really doesn't mean anything. After all, circumcision was around before baptism; should *that* be a prerequisite for observing the Lord's Supper, too!? And, Strong points to John the Baptist's baptism for support, which was not Christian baptism in the full sense at all.

The apostles who first celebrated it had, in all probability, been baptized.

Maybe they were, maybe they weren't. Strong assumes the apostles were all originally John the Baptist's disciples, and because John had probably baptized them, then believer's today should be baptized before observing the Lord's Supper. The New Testament doesn't say this, so the objection doesn't address the point Strong wants to make. At best, he makes the case that believer's baptism is important. I agree.

---

109. Rolland McCune, *A Systematic Theology of Biblical Christianity*, 3 vols. (Detroit: DBTS, 2010), 3:285.

110. Strong (*Systematic*, 971 – 973).

The command of Christ fixes the place of baptism as first in order after discipleship.

Strong quotes from Matthew 28:19; "Go therefore and make disciples of all nations, baptizing them in the name of the Father and of the Son and of the Holy Spirit, teaching them to observe all that I have commanded you …" Jesus told the disciples to (1) make disciples, (2) baptize them, then (3) teach and disciple them. The order means something. Strong remarked that the apostle's practice must be our guide, and they baptized new believers so, by inference, Christians in churches who took the Lord's Supper were baptized.

This is a very good argument! It's clear that Christians must be baptized and, barring some strange set of circumstances, Christians who want to be obedient to the Bible will naturally be baptized church members when they observe the Supper. But, still, this is an inference, not an explicit command. It's more an argument for believer's baptism, than anything else.

All the recorded cases show this to have been the order observed by the first Christians and sanctioned by the apostles.

Again, all Strong demonstrates here is that Christians should be baptized. I agree.

The symbolism of the ordinance requires that baptism should precede the Lord's Supper. The order of the acts signified must be expressed in the order of the ordinances which signify them; else the world is taught that sanctification may take place without regeneration.[111]

Again, this is an inference. Baptism symbolizes a new believer's new birth, and the Lord's Supper is for his sanctification as he awaits

---

111. Strong briefly elaborated on his point, but I omitted it above.

the Lord's return. So, *by inference*, baptism should come first and is a prerequisite. Kiffin argued, "Let all who desire to taste of the sealing power of the second sacrament to nourish them as Saints: First prove the sealing power of the former Sacrament to beget and make you Saints."[112] I agree this principle makes sense, but the New Testament doesn't say it.

Strong also quoted from an ancient Christian document (ca. 2nd century) which reads, "But none shall eat or shall drink from your Eucharist but those baptized in the name of the Lord."[113] This is excellent evidence, and it should be considered. Still, it's not a New Testament command.

The standards of all evangelical denominations, with unimportant exceptions, confirm the view that this is the natural interpretation of the Scripture requirements respecting the order of the ordinances.

This argument sounds good at first, until you realize nearly "all evangelical denominations" baptize unbelieving infants and admit them as church members. So, their reasons for making baptism a prerequisite for the Lord's Supper are irrelevant for Baptist consideration.

The admission of unbaptized persons to the communion tends always to, and has frequently resulted in, the disuse of baptism itself, the obscuring of the truth which it symbolizes, the transformation of Scripturally constituted churches into bodies organized after methods of human invention, and the complete destruction of both church and ordinances as Christ originally constituted them.

---

112. Kiffin (*Sober Discourse*, ch. 3).

113. Rick Brannan, tran., "The Didache," 9.5, in *The Apostolic Fathers in English* (Bellingham: Lexham Press, 2012).

This is hyperbole, and cannot be taken seriously. Strong may have cribbed the argument from Kiffin, who wrote nearly 250 years before him.[114] The fact is that, if a congregation and its pastors want to take a cheap view of church life, they'll do it – whether they practice open communion or not. One does not lead to the other. This is a ridiculous argument. Kiffin has a similar objection.[115]

The Lord's Supper is a church ordinance, observed by churches of Christ as such. For this reason, membership in the church naturally precedes communion. Since communion is a family rite, the participant should first be a member of the family.

A person becomes a member of the New Covenant when she repents of her sins and believes in the Gospel. Church membership is not the same as adoption into God's family, and we should never pretend it is. If we followed Strong's advice, we would doubt somebody was a Christian unless and until she joined a local church. This reasoning runs counter to everything Baptists, the Protestant Reformation and the Bible stand for.

The Lord's Supper is a symbol of church fellowship. Excommunication implies nothing, if it does not imply exclusion from the communion. If the Supper is simply communion of the individual with Christ, then the church has no right to exclude any from it.

---

114. "That swerve from the Lords institutions, and invert his order, has a direct tendency to destroy all modes of worship, and consequently all the public and solemn exercise of religion, in as much as the same reason by which one ordinance may be changed, or discontinued, will equally prove the change or discontinuance of any, year of all at long run," (Kiffin, *Sober Discourse,* ch. 3, summary #3).

115. "For if unbaptized persons may be admitted to all Church privileges, does not such a practice plainly suppose that it is unnecessary? For to what purpose is it to be baptized (may one reason with himself) if he may enjoy all Church privileges without it?" (Kiffin, *Sober Discourse,* ch. 2, section 1).

Again, Strong's argumentation is desperate. He basically asks, if open communion is correct, "then how can a church exclude anybody from the Lord's Supper!?" This is a slippery-slope argument, a boogeyman meant to frighten people into agreement. I'll answer his question with my follow-up remarks (below).

But, Strong is not alone. I'll add two objections to his list from William Kiffin, an early Baptist leader in England:

If unbaptized people can partake of the Lord's Supper, then Baptists look foolish and schismatic![116]

This is ... not the best argument!

"If you ask a rule for baptizing children, may not such a person demand where your rule is for unbaptized persons to receive the Lord's Supper?"[117]

This sounds good at first, but it's actually an empty objection. Kiffin objects that, if you demand, "Show me where it says you can baptize babies!" (and no such Scripture exists), then by what grounds can you defend yourself when an opponent demands, "Show me where it says you can admit unbaptized folks to the Lord's Supper!?"

Well, the Bible teaches the New Covenant is only for believers who've been baptized by the Holy Spirit and experienced regeneration (Mk 1:8; Ezek 36:22-32; Jeremiah 31:31-34). The New Testament only shows us believers being baptized (see ch. 4 for more). So, babies ought not be baptized, because they're not part of the New Covenant!

And, Jesus' own words says unbaptized folks can be admitted to the Lord's Supper. His body was given for His people, and the cup represents the New Covenant in His blood. Believer's baptism has

---

116. Kiffin (*Sober Discourse,* ch. 2, section 2).

117. Kiffin (*Sober Discourse,* ch. 3, section 4).

nothing at all to do with entry into the New Covenant. Kiffin's objection is wrong, and both his questions have been answered.

Summing Up

What is the New Covenant about? What do Jesus' words at its inauguration tell us about who the Supper is for, and what the focus is? What do they tell us about who is eligible to partake? By verbally fencing the table and excluding Christians who aren't church members and aren't baptized by immersion, are we losing focus? Are we keeping the Supper *about the Supper*, or are we shifting it to two other critically important, but different issues?

- Will Jesus drink the fruit of the vine (no doubt, a Welch's kind of fruit!) with New Covenant members, or just with those who have been baptized by immersion and joined a Baptist church?
- Was Jesus' body given for all His elect children, or only for those who have been baptized by immersion and are members of Baptist churches?
- Did Jesus command His disciples to continue observing the Supper in remembrance of His body, which was given for them ... or in remembrance of believer's baptism and local church membership?
- Was Jesus' blood poured out only for believers who have been baptized by immersion and are members in good standing of Baptist churches, or for everyone who is a member of the New Covenant?

At the inauguration of the Supper, what did Jesus say the Supper was about, and who it was for? We've seen the answer, because we've already looked at the text (above) ... and the answer has nothing to do with baptism by immersion by a Baptist minister upon a profession of faith, or local church membership in a Baptist congregation

Suggestions for Local Churches

So, what should a church do? The Bible teaches that (1) believer's baptism is mandatory and expected, (2) church membership is mandatory and expected, (3) the Lord's Supper is for believers only, who are members of the New Covenant. The evidence suggests, by inference, that it's reasonable to expect Christians who partake of the Lord's Supper in local churches to be properly baptized church members. But, Jesus and the Apostle Paul don't say that at all. We may wish they had said it, or suspect it's what they would want, but the Bible doesn't explicitly say this.

So, again, what should a church do? A few things:

1. I suggest a church practice open communion, and allow anyone who is a New Covenant believer to participate.
2. The duty thus falls to parents to ensure their children are regenerate believers *before* they partake of the Supper.
3. Parents can and should consult with their pastors, who can speak to the child. Together, pastors and parents can evaluate the child's faith, and explain the need for believer's baptism if the faith appears to be genuine.
4. When the Supper is observed, a pastor should preface his instructions with a **very** stern call to self-examination about believer's baptism and church membership.
5. I also suggest the following liturgy (or, if you prefer, "order of service") for the Lord's Supper, which can be modified by the reader:

1. **Explanation of the ordinance**

   - Explain the ordinance is for (1) Christians, who are (2) living repentant lives.
   - Explain the need for ongoing repentance and mortification of sin as prerequisites for a faithful Christian life, and urge commitment today.
   - Explain the need for believer's baptism as a prerequisite for a faithful Christian life, and urge commitment today.

2. **Pastoral prayer:**

   This should incorporate both individual and corporate aspects:

   a. **Prayer for the entire congregation:**

   - Almighty God, we also ask you to continually inspire your church around the world with the Spirit of love, unity, and a desire for the truth. We pray that everyone who confesses your holy name may agree in the truth of your holy word, and live in unity and godly love.
   - We ask you to work in the hearts and minds of our elected leaders, that under them we might be governed in a Godly way. We pray our leaders would govern and administer justice with truth and righteousness, and that you would give them the spiritual illumination and conviction to do so. Most of all, we pray for their salvation, and for the salvation of all your chosen people in the world.

   b. **Prayer for individuals:**

   - Almighty God, to whom all hearts are open, all desires known, and from whom no secrets are hid; please cleanse the thoughts of our hearts by the inspiration of your Holy Spirit, that we may perfectly love you, and glorify your holy Name; through Christ our Lord. Amen.

3. **Scripture reading**

   This should be a penitential psalm, a psalm of thanksgiving, or any other appropriate passage that emphasizes salvation, thankfulness, and God's mercy and love.

4. **Distribute and partake of the bread**

   - Explain the symbolism of the bread
   - Pray for the bread (or, even better, ask a member of the congregation to do so).
   - Distribute the bread
   - Read relevant passage from one of the Gospels, or 1 Corinthians 11

- Partake of the bread

5. **Distribute and partake of the cup**

   - Explain the symbolism of the cup
   - Pray for the cup (or, even better, ask a member of the congregation to do so).
   - Distribute the cup
   - Read relevant passage from one of the Gospels, or 1 Corinthians 11
   - Partake of the cup

6. **Sing a hymn to close**

Have the congregation sing a hymn together to close the service.

7: LOCAL CHURCHES GOVERN THEMSELVES

> **SYNOPSIS:**
>
> 1. The evidence from the New Testament shows a trend of local churches moving *away* from centralized command and control to a looser, more autonomous form of governance. Each scheme of church government has some form of Biblical support, but the trend away from centralized organization suggests Congregationalism best fits the evidence.
> 2. Therefore, Baptists believe in a Congregational form of church government, which means:[118]
>   a. The church is self-governing; this is no oversight by any other body.
>   b. The church is independent; there are no obligations produced by denominational alignment or any other outside organization.
>   c. The local church resembles a representative democracy. Members are the ultimate authority in accord with the Word of God, and they elect leaders to fulfill pastoral duties and shepherd the congregation on their behalf.

This is another interesting feature of Baptist life; we believe congregations *govern themselves*, free from oversight and control from outside.[119]

This distinctive goes right to the heart of practical organization and structure. Presbyterians and Methodists, for example, have a bureaucratic structure beyond the local assembly. To be sure, they

---

118. There are adapted from Oats, "GPA 614 – Baptist Policy."

119. Again, you can find a very fair and even-handed discussion of this issue from Erickson (*Christian Theology*, 1079 – 1097).

have their reasons for insisting on this structure. Some Presbyterians believe the situation in Acts 15 (the so-called "Jerusalem Council") is normative for today. That is, local churches getting together to dispute and discuss tricky theological problems, and agreeing to abide by the decisions of the senior ministers once consensus is reached.

One Presbyterian theologian, Robert Reymond, wrote, "Clearly, these congregations were not independent and autonomous. Rather, they were mutually submissive, dependent, and accountable to each other."[120] Likewise, the *Belgic Confession* reads (Article 31.3):[121]

> *It belongeth to synods and councils, ministerially, to determine controversies of faith, and cases of conscience; to set down rules and directions for the better ordering of the public worship of God, and government of his Church; to receive complaints in cases of maladministration, and authoritatively to determine the same: which decrees and determinations, if consonant to the Word of God, are to be received with reverence and submission, not only for their agreement with the Word, but also for the power whereby they are made, as being an ordinance of God, appointed thereunto in his Word.*

Baptists disagree, and believe in an independent, "congregational" form of church government. This means the church runs itself, and the authority within a local church rests with the individual members, led by the elected pastors. Before I begin to describe what "congregationalism" looks like, we'll take a walk through the Book of Acts to see what the bible has to tell us.

A Survey of Church Government from the Book of Acts

---

120. Reymond (*Systematic*, 901).

121. Retrieved from https://reformed.org/documents/index.html.

From Stephen's murder to Paul's first missionary journey

After Stephen's murder, when "there arose on that day a great persecution against the church in Jerusalem," the new Christians scattered around the region to escape (Acts 8:1). One gets the impression of a flight in the dead of night, in great haste, while "Saul was ravaging the church, and entering house after house" to take men off to prison (Acts 8:3). In this context, these newly uprooted Christians "went about preaching the word," (Acts 8:4). This was not a modern church-planting movement, with neatly established polity and close central oversight from the mother church. Instead, what happened was *ad hoc* preachers went about and, empowered by the Spirit, simply preached the Good News.

Philip preached the Gospel in Samaria (Acts 8:5-8), an area some of the Jewish Christians in Jerusalem would have been very reluctant to go. The mother church in Jerusalem promptly sent Peter and John, who mediated the gift of the Holy Spirit to the new believers (Acts 8:14-17). As they headed back home, they preached the gospel to many Samaritans (Acts 8:25). This Samaritan enterprise is more an evangelistic tour than a concerted "church planting" effort.

Philip is later directed by "an angel of the Lord" to preach to an Ethiopian man on his way back south (Acts 8:26-38). The man becomes a believer, Philip is mysteriously carried away by the Holy Spirit, and the Ethiopian "went on his way rejoicing" (Acts 8:39), likely carrying the Good News with him back home. Philip, meanwhile, continued his evangelistic tour up the coast to Caesarea (Acts 8:40). Again, this isn't church planting with a formal church governmental structure; this is simply evangelism.

Paul is converted on the way to Damascus (Acts 9:1-9), intent on finding and arresting the Christians he suspected were lurking in and near the synagogues. Paul was quite right; there *were* Christians there (Acts 9:10, 19, 25). We don't know how they got there, or what their church structure looked like, or what control (if any) the Jerusalem church had over them. What *is* clear is that they had some measure of organization; they masterminded Paul's escape from Damascus and saved his life (Acts 9:23-25). By this time, Luke could speak of "the church throughout all Judea and Galilee and Samaria" (Acts 9:31) but, again, there is no description of a governmental structure.

The Christians who fled from Saul after Stephen's martyrdom "traveled as far as Phoenicia and Cyprus and Antioch," (Acts 11:19). They preached the gospel, and a new congregation at Antioch formed. This is the bible's first indication of a more formal organizational structure outside the church at Jerusalem. The Jerusalem church dispatched Barnabas, who "exhorted them to remain faithful to the Lord with steadfast purpose" (Acts 11:23), then immediately hightailed for Tarsus to find another pastor to help shoulder the load in Antioch. He found Paul, and they ministered to this new congregation together (Acts 11:25-26).

This church now had its own pastors, and made its own decision to send funds for famine relief to their brethren in Judea (Acts 11:29-30). The Holy Spirit spoke to the congregation as a corporate body "while they were worshipping," and directed the Antioch church to appoint its two pastors for a new missionary work (Acts 13:2-3). This is significant, because the Jerusalem church was irrelevant to this decision. There is no indication God mediated this decision through the apostles in Jerusalem, or that they were even informed.

Indeed, Paul and Barnabas acted independently and on their own initiative through this first missionary journey. This is one reason why Baptists believe missionaries should be commissioned by their own local churches. When they returned, Paul and Barnabas made a report back to the congregation at Antioch (Acts 14:26-28).

At this point, the bible shows us the mother church in Jerusalem exercising loose, uncoordinated and inconsistent control over evangelistic and missionary endeavors in the region. The first formal congregation outside Jerusalem is at Antioch, where "the disciples were first called Christians," (Acts 11:26). This church exercises a remarkable degree of autonomy:

1. It's first pastor was appointed by the Jerusalem church.
2. He went to Antioch to fetch another prospective pastor on his own initiative.
3. Together, they led the congregation "for a whole year," (Acts 11:26).
4. The Lord moved the Antioch church to commission its pastors and send them off on an evangelistic trip, without input, consent or delegation from the Jerusalem church.
5. There is no evidence the church at Jerusalem was ever consulted or even notified about this missionary activity
6. Paul and Barnabas acted on their own initiative, and evidently considered themselves deputized by the Antioch church, not the Jerusalem church. They reported back to Antioch upon their return and apparently resumed some or all of their duties with that congregation.

Acts 15 and the so-called "Jerusalem Council"

It's normal in Baptist circles to interpret the so-called Jerusalem Council (Acts 15) as a local church business meeting. One Baptist theologian wrote:

> *Sometimes called the Jerusalem Council, this assembly was not really a church council at all. It was a business meeting of the local church in Jerusalem. The need for the meeting developed when teachers from Jerusalem came to Antioch with the message that circumcision was essential to salvation.*[122]

---

122. Bauder, *Baptist Distinctives*, 97.

If Acts 15 was a church business meeting, then where, pray tell, was the potluck!? I don't think this argument really holds up, but first – a brief survey of the text.

Certain men "from Judea" (not necessarily the Jerusalem church) came down to Antioch and began teaching that people had to follow the Mosaic law (specifically ritual circumcision) in order to be saved (Acts 15:1). Paul wrote against this heresy in the book of Galatians. After Paul and Barnabas "had no small dissension and debate" with these men, the church at Antioch appointed them to head to Jerusalem and go "to the apostles and elders about this question," (Acts 15:2).

It seems Antioch recognized the apostles' inherent authority, and the Jerusalem church's status as the "mother church." A church plant naturally looks up to the parent church. The leaders in Antioch looked up to the apostles in Jerusalem. They sought advice and consensus.

They arrived in Jerusalem and "were welcomed by the church and the apostles and the elders," (Acts 15:4). Paul and Barnabas explained how God's grace had clearly gone out to the Gentiles. This was too much for some of the Christians "who belonged to the party of the Pharisees." They protested, "it is necessary to circumcise them, and to charge them to keep the law of Moses," (Acts 15:5).

The fight was on. It's interesting that James and the others in the Jerusalem church *had* to know this was simmering below the surface, yet they apparently did nothing. The Jerusalem church was always characterized by a velvet-glove approach to this issue (cf. Acts 21:20-25).

The Jerusalem congregation did not gather to hash this out; only "the apostles and elders" did (Acts 15:6). "Much debate" ensued (Acts 15:7). Peter spoke (Acts 15:7-11). Paul and Barnabas gave testimony (Acts 15:12). Then James issued his judgment; "we should not trouble those of the Gentiles who turn to God," (Acts 15:19).

James didn't mention *Antioch*. He mentioned "Gentiles" in a generic sense, indicating he was speaking to a much larger issue. The dispute in Antioch was the impetus for a decision which had implications far beyond that single city. The letter the council then sent with Paul and Barnabas for distribution was not for Antioch; it was for the *entire region* encompassing "the brethren who are of the Gentiles in Antioch and Syria and Cilicia," (Acts 15:23). This was a circular letter.

The letter read, "it seemed good to the Holy Spirit and to us to lay upon you no greater burden than these necessary things . . ." (Acts 15:28). This is not the language of a friendly suggestion. It reads like the language of a friendly ecclesiastical *superior* to an *inferior*. A Pastor of a church cannot "lay upon you" a burden to another church. He *can* offer friendly advice. This is not what happened here.

The Dogma of Acts 16:4

If Acts 15 simply depicts a Baptist church business meeting (minus the casserole and the fried chicken), then why does Acts 16:4 read thus:

> As they went on their way through the cities, they delivered to them for observance **the decisions which had been reached** by the apostles and elders who were at Jerusalem (Acts 16:4).

This is strong language. Paul and Timothy are passing through Syria and Cilicia (Acts 15:41), apparently revisiting "the brethren in every city where we proclaimed the word of the Lord," (Acts 15:36). As they passed through these cities, they "delivered to them for observance the decisions which had been reached by the apostles and elders who were at Jerusalem," (Acts 16:4).

It's very possible this circular letter hadn't yet reached the region beyond Antioch. Paul and Timothy were making sure it did. Notice the language Luke used. This letter is not a suggestion. The Greek word is *dogma,* a word you likely recognize. It's an *ordinance*, an *order*, a *decree*. It was a decision reached by the "apostles and elders" at Jerusalem. It carried authority. It was "delivered to them for observance." Does Acts 15 still sound like a local church business meeting?

To make matters worse, the word the RSV and ESV translate as "decisions" is actually *much* stronger than that. It was more than a decision; it was an order. The KJV, for example, uses the word "decrees." The phrase here is τὰ δόγματα ("the dogma"). The phrase is well attested in the Septuagint (the Greek translation of the Old Testament used by Jesus and the early church), the New Testament and the early post-apostolic era. The phrase encompasses the concepts of *decree, ordinance* or *doctrine*.[123] For example:

- *In the LXX*, we read that Nebuchadnezzar issued a decree (i.e. an **order**) that all the wise men of Babylon be brought forth, to interpret his dream (LXX Daniel 4:3). Later, Darius issued a decree (i.e. a **law**) that no man could pray to anyone except him for 30 days (LXX Daniel 6:9; see also 6:11, 13, 14, 16, 27).
- *In the NT*, we read about the decree (i.e. an **order**) which went out from Caesar Augustus that all the world must be taxed (Lk 2:1). The Jews in Thessalonica claimed Paul and his companions were advocating for another king, in violation of Caesar's decrees (i.e. **laws**; Acts 17:7). Paul wrote that Christ abolished "the law of commandments and ordinances," (i.e. **regulations**; Eph 2:15). He also stated that Christ "canceled

---

123. For a full discussion, see Moises Silva, *New International Dictionary of New Testament Theology and Exegesis,* 5 vols. (Grand Rapids: Zondervan, 2014), 1:752-753.

Kittell wrote that "In Ac. 16:4 the word signifies the resolutions and decrees of the early church in Jerusalem which are to be sent out to the cities of the first missionary journey. In the post-apostolic fathers the word comes to be applied to the teachings and prescriptions of Jesus," (Gerhard Kittel, "δόγμα, δογματίζω," in *Theological Dictionary of the New Testament*, ed. Gerhard Kittel, Geoffrey W. Bromiley and Gerhard Friedrich [Grand Rapids: Eerdmans, 1964–], 2:231).

the bond which stood against us with its legal demands" (i.e. **regulations**; Col 2:14).
- *In the early post-apostolic era*, Ignatius wrote that Christians must "be diligent therefore to be confirmed in the ordinances (i.e. **commands, orders**)[124] of the Lord and the Apostles," (*Magnesians* 13.1). Barnabas wrote, "there are then three doctrines (i.e. **teachings, commands**) of the Lord," (*Epistle* 1.6). The *Didache* reads, "and concerning the Apostles and Prophets, act thus according to the ordinance (i.e. **command, order**) of the Gospel," (11.3).

So, how should we understand "the dogma" which Paul and Timothy delivered for observance to these churches? It's clear from this short survey that something anemic like "decision" is a poor fit. It is doubtful the translation *law* will do; the Jerusalem Council was not a civil body with legislative authority. Perhaps *regulation* or *ordinance* is best. To be even more blunt, perhaps we can bring things down to the bottom shelf, so to speak, and drop *ordinance* in favor of *order*. After all, the very English word "ordinance" means an authoritative decree or a law.[125]

It appears this was not a suggestion from the Jerusalem Council; it was a *decree*, an *order*. Some might seek to soften it and say *decision*, but I don't believe you can escape the fact that the Jerusalem church exercised a unique power and status in the early Christian era.

The second missionary journey

---

124. Michael Holmes (*The Apostolic Fathers,* 2nd ed. [Grand Rapids: Baker, 1989]) translated this as "precepts."

125. *Merriam-Webster Collegiate Dictionary*, 11th ed. (Springfield: Merriam-Webster, 2003), s.v. "ordinance," 1a, 1b.

There are Christians ("brothers") at Lystra and Iconium (Acts 16:1-2), and individual "churches" in the region that "increased in numbers daily" (Acts 16:5), but we have no idea how they developed or what governmental structure they employed.

Paul, Barnabas and Luke apparently started a new congregation at Philippi when Lydia and her household were converted (Acts 16:11-15). Luke referred to them as "brothers" when they later passed through the city on their way to Thessalonica (Acts 16:40). When Paul and Silas faced a hostile crowd in Thessalonica (Acts 17:1-9), Luke tells us "the brothers" (Acts 17:10) immediately spirited them away. It's uncertain whether these "brothers" were other members of the missionary party, or a small group of Christians in Thessalonica. The situation is the same in Berea (Acts 17:14).

Paul made a few converts in Athens (Acts 17:34), then spent a year and a half in Corinth, where he planted a church and taught the congregation (Acts 18:1-11). By this time, there was apparently a congregation in Caesarea (Acts 18:22) which Paul visited after he passed through Ephesus on his return to Antioch.

Paul's second missionary journey has no insight for us about church government. Churches are multiplying and the gospel is spreading, but Luke didn't record anything relevant about polity.

Third missionary journey

By this time, there are apparently churches throughout the regions of Galatia and Phrygia, in modern-day Turkey (Acts 18:23). Paul spent two years in Ephesus, where he planted a church and engaged in aggressive evangelism, "so that all the residents of Asia heard the word of the Lord, both Jews and Greeks," (Acts 19:10). Paul later sent Timothy and Erastus ahead of him on a missionary sweep through Macedonia (Acts 19:22). He dealt with a near riot in Ephesus because his ministry was so successful (Acts 19:23-41), then left that congregation and headed for Macedonia to join his friends (Acts 20:1).

On his return, Paul made sure to meet with the elders of the church at Ephesus, to encourage them as he made his way to Jerusalem (Acts 20:17). There were apparently Christians at Tyre, whom they visited (Acts 21:7), along with the church at Caesarea (Acts 21:16). Paul made it to Jerusalem, where he was arrested.

Summary of the evidence from the book of Acts

The Book of Acts shows us the mother church in Jerusalem exercising early, loose, uncoordinated and inconsistent control over evangelistic and missionary endeavors. The key passage is clearly Acts 15, which shows the Jerusalem church exercising a Presbyterian-style church polity. However, Luke doesn't provide any further hints or details about church polity for the rest of the book.

In fact, the Book of Acts doesn't seem interested in giving us a clear picture of church government.[126] Some Baptists, in their zeal to defend congregational church government, overstate the case. We've just surveyed the case and it's weak all around, for every form of church government:

- Folks who advocate for a more dictatorial, Episcopal form of government have to explain who is in charge, and why he's in charge, and why *someone else* isn't!
- Presbyterians have to go beyond Acts 15, and explain where their system is in Acts 16-28. They have to explain how the mother church in Jerusalem exercised representative control over local churches in Macedonia or Asia. And, if they believe regional synods were formed to do just that, where the bible says this!

---

126. Millard Erickson was correct when he wrote, "It is probably safe to say that the evidence from the New Testament is inconclusive; nowhere in the New Testament do we find a picture closely resembling any of the fully developed systems of today," (*Christian Theology,* 1094).

- Congregationalists have to try and downplay the implications of Acts 15 which, as we've already seen, is very hard to do! They often heavily emphasize the independent decisions of local churches, and downplay the implications of the Jerusalem church's clear control in the earliest chapters of the Book of Acts.

What Form of Church Government is Biblical?

The best thing to do in light of the evidence is to consider *what direction* the situation was headed in, and what the Bible tells us about the capabilities and responsibilities of church members.[127]

It's clear the trend was going towards de-centralized, independent churches. It would have been impossible for the apostles to implement and pull off a centralized church government structure from Jerusalem. The Book of Acts, at the end, shows us Christian congregations scattered throughout Judea, Samaria, Asia and Macedonia. The evidence from Antioch suggests an independent church polity developed either by design or expediency. It appears congregations governed themselves during this time, but would certainly listen and obey the apostles in Jerusalem if they had reason (or the ability) to hear from them.

Each New Testament author wrote his letters to individual congregations with advice, admonition and instruction for them. There are no references to a higher ecclesiastical authority, other than the writer's occasional reference to his own office as an apostle. In giving their advice and encouragement, the New Testament authors assume churches will act independently to implement this advice.

Discipline of unruly church members is a local affair, not something a higher authority has right to intervene in (e.g. 1 Cor 5). Paul makes references to individual churches collecting money for

---

127. Erickson (*Christian Theology* 1095 – 1096).

famine relief (2 Cor 8-9), without instruction from Jerusalem. And, to borrow an anecdote from the immediate post-apostolic era, the *Book of 1 Clement* shows us one local church (Rome) sending a corporate letter of concern to another assembly (Corinth) with brotherly advice.[128]

It's true the early chapters of the Book of Acts show a more centralized, loose command and control. But, this situation *is not* normative for today. The apostles are dead, and they have no successors (see the discussion about apostles, in ch. 8). There is no First Baptist Church of Jerusalem. Instead, the Book of Acts shows us a movement away from centralized command and control towards every assembly being accountable for itself, and directly responsible to Christ as its head. Because every Christian is a priest for God (see ch. 9), and personally responsible for what he believes and what he does (see ch. 10), then congregational government best fits the biblical evidence.

Michael Bird, an Anglican theologian, wrote, "all models of church government can be anchored in the biblical material to some degree."[129] He's right, but the *trajectory* is away from centralization. This is why Congregational government (described further in the next chapter) is the best choice. However, we should remember something else Bird noted:[130]

> *One thing I have learned is this: the single most important factor in the governance of the church is not the structure or*

---

128. The opening salutation reads, "The church of God which temporarily resides in Rome, to the church of God which temporarily resides in Corinth, those who are called and sanctified by the will of God through our Lord Jesus Christ. Grace and peace from Almighty God through Jesus Christ be multiplied to you." Likewise, the post-script reads, "The letter of the Romans to the Corinthians," (Brannan, *Apostolic Fathers*).

129. Bird (*Evangelical Theology*, KL 17054).

130. Bird (*Evangelical Theology*, KL 17054).

model it is based on, but the Christian character of the folks who lead it.

What is "congregational government?"

We believe each church is individually accountable to God. And, for these same reasons, Baptists also believe the New Covenant scriptures teach us the people in a congregation are directly involved in the government and management of the local church.

Baptist church government is called "congregationalism" because, well . . . we believe the folks in the church run the church. However, this isn't a strict democracy.[131] It's more of a republican form of government, where the people appoint and elect their own leaders to fulfill the New Covenant offices of responsibility (pastor and deacon), let those leaders operate, and **hold them accountable** to do so in a Biblical, Christ-honoring way.

> *In other words, a local church that is ordered according to the New Testament will have two centers of authority. One the one hand, the congregation will possess the authority and bear the responsibility of making decisions about the church's leadership, membership, policies, direction, and programs. As a member of the church, the pastor is obligated to submit to the authority of the congregation.*
>
> *On the other hand, the pastor will possess the authority to preach, teach, apply, and illustrate the Word of God. Whenever he faithfully and accurately brings the Scriptures to bear upon life, the congregation is obliged to obey him. Furthermore, when the congregation makes decisions, it must do more than count votes. It must weigh counsel, and the*

---

131. For an excellent discussion of congregational government, see Bauder (*Baptist Distinctives*, 91-128).

> *pastor's counsel (informed by the Scriptures and reinforced by his example) ought to weigh very heavily. The church submits by listening carefully, evaluating the pastor's teachings in the light of God's Word and, where they are accurate, obeying.*[132]

This is important. Congregationalism has the people holding the leadership responsible, while also obeying that leadership. "The authority of pastors is moral —depending on their character, their call from God, their Christian knowledge, and their position as religious teachers."[133] However, Presbyterianism (or example) believes God invests divine authority in the elders, *not the assembly*.[134]

Some Presbyterians believe a Congregational form of government has a "disintegrative effect" and doesn't reflect the unity Christian congregations should have as the one body of Christ.[135] Others believe it implies a "rejection of all meaningful connectionalism between local Christian bodies."[136] This is the kind of well-intentioned rhetoric which has no teeth. Baptists believe in cooperative fellowship and a joint approach to Gospel ministry; we just won't abdicate the autonomy of a local church to a larger bureaucracy.

Baptists have always believed this. For example, John Smyth, who started perhaps the first "Baptist" congregation in the earliest years of the 17th century, wrote in his own confession of faith that churches

---

132. Bauder (*Baptist Distinctives,* 109).

133. Hovey (*Systematic,* 310). He continued, and offered this thoughtful remark, "Probably ministers do not have as much control over their people as the New Testament authorizes them to have; but it is because they are not sufficiently wise and godly to win it."

134. See especially Berkhof (*Systematic,* 584).

135. Berkhof (*Systematic,* 580–581).

136. Reymond (*Systematic,* 907).

have authority to preach the word, administer the sacraments (etc.), "but the last appeal is to the brethren or body of the church."[137] Likewise, the Particular Baptists in London in 1644 wrote that a local assembly elected its own officers, "and that none other have power to impose them, either these or any other."[138]

It's interesting that the 1833 *New Hampshire Confession of Faith* didn't bother to define "the church" in a catholic, corporate way; it simply focused on the local congregation ("we believe that a visible Church of Christ is a congregation of baptized believers …").[139] This reflects a Baptist distinctive; the local congregation is where the rubber meets the road.

Likewise, the latest version of the Southern Baptist Convention's *Faith and Message* reads, "a New Testament church of the Lord Jesus Christ is an autonomous **local congregation** of baptized believers …"[140]

The GARBC's *Articles of Faith* have a very strong expression of local church autonomy:[141]

> … We hold that the local church has the absolute right of self-government free from the interference of any hierarchy of individuals or organizations; and that the one and only Superintendent is Christ through the Holy Spirit; that it is Scriptural for true churches to cooperate with each other in contending for the faith and for the furtherance of the gospel; that each local church is the sole judge of the measure and

---

137. Lumpkin, "Short Confession of Faith in 20 Articles (1609)" Article 13, in *Baptist Confessions*, 101.

138. Lumpkin, "London Confession (1644)," Article 36, in *Baptist Confessions,* 166.

139. 1833 *New Hampshire Confession of Faith*, Article 13.

140. Southern Baptist Convention, *2000 Baptist Faith and Message,* Article 6. Emphasis added.

141. GARBC, *Articles of Faith,* Article 14. Revised 2014.

> *method of its cooperation; that on all matters of membership, of polity, of government, of discipline, of benevolence, the will of the local church is final.*

To be sure, all true Christians who have repented of their rebellion against God, and believed in who Jesus and what He's done have been regenerated by the Spirit and been adopted into God's family. But, to be a "Baptist" means you're committed to a *particular idea* of what the church is, and how it should be run – because the Bible teaches it.

You may not really care about all this. You may just love the Lord, and want to worship Him. You might prefer to leave doctrine to "other people." This sentiment is understandable, but terribly wrong. If you're a Christian, you have the indwelling Spirit to guide you, unique and important gifts to exercise, and wisdom which deserves to be heard. Baptists believe all members of the congregation ought to be involved in serving, and that includes the decisions which determine where the church is going.

As one author noted, "The Baptist recognizes the plurality of the gifts bestowed upon their churches, believing that each and every member has a God-given capability to contribute to the total ministry of the fellowship to its own members and to the world in proclaiming the gospel."[142]

And, Congregational government has at least two added benefits:[143]

1. It helps protect a congregation from rottenness and apostasy at the larger, higher level.

---

142. Hoad (*The Baptist,* 230).

143. Hammett (*Biblical Foundations,* 150-151).

Bureaucracies are excellent vehicles for heresy, especially if they go bad at the regional or national level. Some conservative Presbyterian congregations, for example, have found themselves in costly lawsuits with their regional bureaucracies when they attempt to leave apostate denominations.

2. An involved congregation is a thriving congregation.

The more the members are actively involved in planning and carrying out their business, guided by wise and skilled leaders, the more committed they are.

We want to do God's work God's way, and we believe that way is summed up by commitments to (1) local church autonomy, (2) the congregation's independence from any higher authority than Christ, and (3) a belief in a congregational form of church government.

8: THE ONLY CHURCH OFFICERS ARE PASTORS AND DEACONS

SYNOPSIS:

1. The office of "apostle" ended with the 12 original apostles, and Paul.
2. The titles "pastor," "elder" and "bishop/overseer" are synonymous and capture different facets of the elder's Biblical job description.
3. A pastor doesn't have to be a superstar; he just has to be competent. His duties are these:
    a. to preach the word and "tend the flock of God that is [his] charge."
    b. to administer all the ordinances of the Gospel which belong to his sacred office
    c. to be faithful and diligent in his office
    d. to care for his congregation
    e. to be an example
    f. to never play favorites
    g. to be a leader, not a dictator
4. There must be two or more pastors in a local congregation
5. Because there are no church officers above the local congregation, a Congregational form of government is the best.

The apostles are dead, they don't have any successors, so the only church officers are those of (1) a local pastor and (2) a deacon. Many other churches don't agree, and teach that there is a bureaucratic level (and bureaucratic people, too) above the local church. Again, the New Testament is our guide.

The Office of an Apostle

The Greek word our English Bibles translate as "apostle" really just refers to someone with special and extraordinary status, who's been commissioned and sent on a particular mission. Like the word "baptize," it's a Greek word we've imported over into English.

The Gospels tells us the 12 apostles were men who Jesus specifically chose, appointed, commissioned and sent out to evangelize the Jewish people. He trained them to form the nucleus of the church in Jerusalem after He left. Jesus told the apostles, "you shall receive power when the Holy Spirit has come upon you; and you shall be my witnesses in Jerusalem and in all Judea and Samaria and to the end of the earth," (Acts 1:8). The original apostles are referred to by that title a combined 10 times in all four Gospels (Mt 10:2; Mk 3:14, 6:30; Lk 6:13, 9:10, 11:49, 17:5, 22:14, 24:10 and Jn 13:16).

In the Book of Acts, we clearly see the apostles fulfilling this unique, protectorate role. They led the church and directed its ministry efforts. They ministered the Gospel to the crowds at Pentecost (Acts 2:37). They taught in the church together (Acts 2:42) and had the power to perform miraculous signs (Acts 2:43; 5:12). They testified about how they'd personally witnessed Jesus' resurrection (Acts 4:33), and they collected community offerings (Acts 4:35, 37; 5:2). They even provided new names to believers (Acts 4:36)!

The apostles foreknew when God would strike people dead (Acts 5:1-11). The Jewish leaders recognized the apostles as Jesus' special envoys *extraordinaire* (Acts 5:17, 27-32), and "filled with jealousy they arrested the apostles and put them in the common prison," (Acts 5:17-18). They were rescued from prison by angelic intervention, and were ordered to preach the Gospel in public, defying the apostate Israelites who'd put them in jail (Acts 5:19-20).

The apostles were the ones who ordained the first deacons (Acts 6:1-6). They're the ones who bravely stayed in Jerusalem when Saul began his systematic persecution of the Christian church, while their congregation fled (Acts 8:1). They mediated the baptism of the Holy Spirit to the new Christians in Samaria (Acts 8:14-16). Barnabas recognized their authority, and brought Paul to them shortly after his conversion to assure them he was now a true believer (Acts 9:27).

Barnabas is called an apostle twice, along with Paul (Acts 14:4, 14). There is no record of Barnabas having the apostolic sign gifts. The apostles are the ones the church in Antioch sent Paul and Barnabas to, for advice about whether Gentiles had to follow Jewish laws in order to be "true Christians," (Acts 15:2). By this point, the apostles were a distinct group from the elders (i.e. pastors) of the church in Jerusalem (see Acts 15:4, 6, 22-23). The Bible doesn't tell us why; perhaps the elders took care of the Jerusalem church and the apostles focused their energies on the needs of the ever-growing body of Christ in the region. Yet, the apostles *and* the elders at the Jerusalem church exercised unique control over other churches. Paul and Barnabas left the meeting in Jerusalem, visited many churches and "delivered to them for observance the decisions which had been reached by the apostles and elders who were at Jerusalem," (Acts 16:4).

Paul identifies himself as an apostle many times in his letters (Rom 1:1; Rom 11:13; 1 Cor 1:1; 1 Cor 9:1; 1 Cor 15:9; 2 Cor 1:1; Gal 1:1; Eph 1:1; Col 1:1; 1 Tim 1:1; 1 Tim 2:7; 2 Tim 1:1, 11; Titus 1:1). Peter did the same (1 Pet 1:1; 2 Pet 1:1). Paul understood only very few men held the office of "apostle," which is clear by the way he told the church at Rome that two Christians were "men of note among the apostles," (Rom 16:7; see also 1 Cor 9:5).

Paul suggests that Apollos *might* have been considered an apostle (see 1 Cor 3:1 – 4:9), but doesn't specifically say this. He also suggested the same thing about Timothy and Silvanus (1 Thess 2:6; the "we" is identified in 1 Thess 1:1). He recognized this is a God-ordained office (1 Cor 12:28), but didn't suggest every church has an apostle. He only said God has appointed apostles "in the church," meaning the "big church" I spoke about earlier. He explained that

Jesus took special care to show His resurrected self to the apostles (1 Cor 15:7).

It's clear the office of "apostle" was very special and unique, because false teachers soon began claiming *to be* apostles themselves (2 Cor 11:5, 13; 2 Cor 12:11; Rev 2:2)! The "signs of a true apostle" (2 Cor 12:12) seem to be the miraculous sign gifts. Paul said the apostles are the ones to whom the mystery of full Gentile inclusion into God's family was revealed (Eph 3:5).

And, Paul tells us the household of God (that is, the "big church") is built on the twin foundations of the Old Covenant prophets and the New Testament apostles, with Christ Himself being the chief cornerstone (Eph 2:20).[144] Indeed, Peter also obliquely referred to these same "pillars" when he warned the churches in his second circular letter to "remember the predictions of the holy prophets and the commandment of the Lord and Savior through your apostles," (2 Pet 3:2) about false teachers. Jude echoed this sentiment (Jude 17). Finally, in the New Jerusalem, the names of the 12 apostles will be engraved on the foundation stones of the city wall (Rev 21:14).

In this brief survey, I have mentioned *every single reference* to "apostles" in the entire New Testament. We can make some brief conclusions from this data:

1. Apostles were chosen by Jesus Christ to be His *envoys extraordinaire* to the world. Judas was replaced by Paul, who affirmed his status many, many times in the New Testament.
2. Apostles performed apostolic sign gifts of healing and miracle-working.
3. Apostles have a parallel status with the Old Covenant prophets, and with them are the twin pillars of the church
4. Luke directly referred to Barnabas as an apostle, and Paul indirectly suggests Timothy and Silvanus are apostles.

---

144. Many commentators believe Paul is referring to New Covenant apostles. I disagree.

However, none of the three were chosen by Christ, none ever had apostolic sign gifts, and none were ever granted favored status in the New Testament.

In conclusion, there is nothing in the New Testament about the apostolic office continuing beyond the 12. We know this, because I just reviewed *every single time* the word occurred in the New Testament, and that teaching isn't there. This suggests that, if someone claims to hold a position *above* that of a pastor of a local church, you ought to raise a skeptical, polite eyebrow … or perhaps two.

The Office of the Pastor

The title of the "pastor"

Some people believe Christians borrowed the office of "elder" from the Jewish synagogue, but that's unlikely. "The New Testament church borrowed *the title*, and the official status that came along with that title, more than the specific duties that those who held this title performed."[145]

There are three terms in the New Testament which refer to what a pastor does. He is a "pastor" in the same that he's a shepherd of a flock of Christians (Acts 20:20, 27-30; Eph 4:11; 1 Pet 5:2, 4). He's a "guardian" or "bishop" in the sense that he protects his congregation from spiritual harm, as an overseer (Acts 20:28-29; Phil 1:1; 1 Tim. 3:2; Titus 1:7; 1 Pet 2:25). He's also an "elder," in the sense that he's in charge of the congregation, in some sense (1 Tim. 5:17; Acts 11:30).

---

145. Benjamin Merkle, "The Scriptural Basis for Elders," in *Baptist Foundations* (KL 4332-4333).

All of these terms are synonymous, and refer to the same office.[146] This is why, for example, the Apostle Peter could write this sentence which encapsulates *all three* of these duties into the one office:

> So I exhort the **<u>elders</u>** among you, as a fellow elder and a witness of the sufferings of Christ, as well as a partaker in the glory that is going to be revealed: **<u>shepherd the flock</u>** of God that is among you, **<u>exercising oversight</u>**, not under compulsion, but willingly, as God would have you ..." (1 Pet 5:1-2a).

So, these different titles describe complementary roles for the same office. A church could use the title "elder" or "pastor" to refer to its leaders. "Bishop" might not be the best choice, though!

The job of the pastor

Every Pastor grows depressed when he reads books about "how to be a better Pastor." I believe that, if a pastor took five popular "how to be a Pastor" books by conservative authors, and compiled a list of everything these books said, he'd be one depressed guy. Of course, not all of these lists are credible.

For example, one well-known Christian leader recently posted, on Twitter, that one "warning sign" of a bad pastor is that has a "poor social media witness." No, I'm not joking. Somehow, I must have missed that requirement in the Bible. Yes, now that I think on it ... I'm almost certain the Apostle Paul mentioned a weekly quota for FaceBook, Twitter and Instagram posts!

That madness aside, these lists can be depressing. No doubt about it. But, I want to offer a small ray of sunshine. When it comes to

---

146. On this point, see especially R. W. Dale, *Congregational Church Polity* (London, UK: Hodder & Stoughton, 1885), 91 – 94. See also Merkle ("Scriptural Basis," in *Baptist Foundations,* KL 4363 - 4427).

pastoral requirements, I don't believe God requires a man to be perfect at everything. He asks for competence, not brilliance; along with a willingness to get better and learn over time.

Let me use a sports analogy. In baseball, the "ideal" athlete is known as a "five-tool player." This means a guy who can (1) hit for power, (2) hit for a good average, (3) has good base-running skills and speed, (4) can throw, and (5) can field. Most guys aren't "five-tool players." Most baseball players can do one or more of these things very well, and are competent at the rest. A superstar is generally someone who can do all five.

Some Pastors are "five-tool" guys. They can do everything very, very well. Most guys can't do that. And, I don't think God asks for brilliance. But, I think He does expect competence. So, what's the basic job of a pastor? I'll make this relatively brief, but I believe this discussion is comprehensive enough to get the point across.[147]

1. **The Pastor must preach the word and "tend the flock of God that is [his] charge," (1 Pet 5:2).**

The Pastor's job is to systematically, steadily preach God's word to his people, and to teach them everything that Jesus has commanded them. This work encompasses both the Old and New Covenant scriptures; "he must make known the whole Counsel of God to the People."[148]

The pastor should take this responsibility very seriously. "If someone speaks, [do it like he's speaking] God's [very] words," (1 Pet

---

147. I've adapted this list from Benjamin Keach, *The Glory of a True Church and its Discipline display'd Wherein a true Gospel-Church is described. Together with the Power of the Keys, and who are to be let in, and who to be shut out* (London, UK: John Robinson, 1697). My edition was reprinted in Mark Dever (ed.), *Polity: Biblical Arguments on How to Conduct Church Life* (Washington, D.C.: Center for Church Reform, 2001), 63 - 92. This excerpt is on pg. 66.

148. Ibid, 66.

4:11).[149] His job is to speak and teach God's words, not his own. The Apostle Peter's command speaks to the attitude and mindset pastors bring to the pulpit.

2. **A pastor's job is to administer all the ordinances of the Gospel which belong to his sacred office.**

The ordinance of believer's baptism pictures and shows the inward spiritual reality of a sinner saved by grace, washed of her sins, and united with Christ's death to sin and resurrection to new life, by the baptism of the Holy Spirit. It's the initiatory rite into a local congregation, and displays "in a solemn and beautiful emblem, our faith in the crucified, buried, and risen Saviour, with its effect in our death to sin and resurrection to a new life."[150]

Likewise, the Lord's Supper is an ordinance of renewal, and a beautiful vehicle for growth in Christ. As Christians partake of the bread and wine, they "commemorate together the dying love of Christ; preceded always by solemn self-examination."[151] They also remember His miraculous resurrection, by which He defeated Satan for sinners, in their place, as their representative. They're also reminded to watch and wait for His return.

These ordinances are symbols and object lessons for precious Gospel truths, and they're also God-ordained vehicles for sanctification and grace. The ordinances don't *channel* God's grace to us in some mystical fashion. But, like a powerful sermon, they're vehicles for growth in Christ to the extent we observe them with

---

149. This is my own translation.

150. 1833 *New Hampshire Confession of Faith* (Article 14).

151. Ibid.

renewed and re-dedicated faith in Christ and His Gospel.[152] It's a pastor's job to observe these ordinances in a sacred, holy and reverent way, and to teach the congregation to do the same.

3. A pastor's job is to be faithful and diligent in his office.

The Apostle Paul told Timothy, "Do your best to present yourself to God as one approved, a workman who has no need to be ashamed, rightly handling the word of truth," (2 Tim 2:15). This is good advice. A pastor must be engaged, busy and laboring in his office. If Jesus returned tomorrow, the pastor shouldn't have reason to be ashamed of his efforts and energies for the flock God has given him. As he labors, he must be careful to "rightly handle" the word of truth. Every Christian is responsible for what he does with the foundation he has in Christ Jesus (see 1 Cor 3:10-15); including a pastor.

4. A pastor's job is to care for his congregation.

The pastors of a church should deliberately get to know the people, to know their spiritual state. He should watch out for them, inquire into their spiritual life, offer to pray for them, strengthen those who are struggling, comfort those who are struggling with sins, and to rebuke those who are living in unrepentant and deliberate sin.

He should "pray for them at all times, and with them also when sent for, and desired, and as Opportunity serves; and to sympathize with them in every State and Condition, with all Love and Compassion."[153]

---

152. Erickson remarked, "We might say, then, that it is not so much that the sacrament brings Christ to the communicant as that the believer's faith brings Christ to the sacrament," (*Christian Theology,* 1128 – 1129).

153. Keach, in Dever (*Polity,* 66).

5. A pastor's job is to be an example.

Some Christians think a pastor should be sinless. They might not literally *say* this, but some people basically believe that. Let me assure you; a pastor is a human being like anyone else. He gets angry. He gets frustrated. He can be petty. He can be spiteful. He can be rude. In short, he's just like you.

When you think about the "pastoral qualifications" from 1 Timothy 3 and Titus 1, you shouldn't view them as a checklist. We're all sinners, and a pastor is an undeserving recipient of salvation, just like you. Instead, these requirements are more about general moral character than anything else. "Can this person serve as an example in this crucial area of life? That is the question."[154]

Don't *tsk, tsk* if a pastor seems short with his son once or twice. Don't raise your eyebrows when, after a very long morning at church, a pastor seems a *bit* ill-tempered with his wife. You've done the same, and you know it. What is his pattern of life? What is his general character? Yes, he's not perfect; nobody but Jesus is (see Gal 2:21). But, can he be an example of how to manage his household? Is he an example of how to keep his children submissive and faithful to his authority? Does he model how to love his wife, just as Christ loves the church? Does he have an upright and holy way of life?

In short, a pastor's job isn't to be perfect. I'm quite convinced that, for some people, if Jesus Christ Himself showed up at their church on Sunday morning and began to preach from the pulpit, some folks in the congregation would find something to complain about! No, a pastor's job is to, "as near as he can, *[be]* a good Example in Conversation, Charity, Faith and Purity; that his Ministry may be the more acceptable to all, and the Name of God be glorified, and Religion delivered from Reproach."[155]

---

154. Hammett (*Biblical Foundations,* 168).

155. Keach, in Dever (*Polity,* 66).

6. **A pastor must never play favorites.**

"He must see he carries it to all with all Impartiality, not preferring the Rich above the Poor."[156]

7. **A pastor must be a leader, not a dictator.**

Peter wrote (1 Pet 5:2-5),

> *Tend the flock of God that is your charge, not by constraint but willingly, not for shameful gain but eagerly, not as domineering over those in your charge but being examples to the flock. And when the chief Shepherd is manifested you will obtain the unfading crown of glory.*
>
> *Likewise you that are younger be subject to the elders.*
>
> *Clothe yourselves, all of you, with humility toward one another, for "God opposes the proud, but gives grace to the humble."*

There are many other lists floating around which describe the pastor's job.[157] But these get to the heart of the issue.

Qualifications of a pastor

---

156. Ibid.

157. For example, one recent book listed seven core responsibilities; (1) preaching and teaching the Word of God, (2) administration in the church, (3) shepherding the flock, (4) biblical counseling, (5) evangelizing, (6) making disciples and (7) visioneering (Jim Vogel [ed.], *The Pastor: A Guide for God's Faithful Servant* [Schaumberg: Regular Baptist Press, 2012]).

The classic passages about pastoral qualifications are from 1 Timothy and Titus. Rather than discuss each qualification, I'll provide a comparison of the two passages and what they say:

	1 Timothy 3:1-7	Titus 1:6-9
Above reproach	X	X
"One woman man"	X	X
Sober-minded	X	
Self-controlled	X	X
Respectable	X	
Hospitable	X	X
Able to teach	X	
Not a drunkard	X	X
Not violent but gentle	X	X
Not quarrelsome	X	
Not a lover of money	X	X
Manage his household well	X	
Keep children submissive with all dignity	X	
Not a recent convert	X	
Well thought of by outsiders	X	
Children are believers ("faithful") and have good conduct		X
Not arrogant		X
Not quick-tempered		X
A lover of good		X
Upright		X
Holy		X
Disciplined		X
Holds firm to the Word		X

In addition to this list, the book of 2 Timothy also contains some important implications for pastoral ministry:

1. He must be a leader, not a coward (2 Tim 1:3-7)
2. He must be committed to the Bible (2 Tim 1:13)

3. He must be educated, competent and capable – so he can guard the faith (2 Tim 1:14)[158]
4. He must be able to train new leaders (2 Tim 2:1-2)
5. He must be totally committed to the Gospel ministry (2 Tim 2:3-10)
6. He must not preach a cheap Gospel, and must encourage self-examination (2 Tim 2:11-14a)
7. He must be theologically balanced and mature (2 Tim 2:14b – 18)[159]
8. He must be spiritually and emotionally mature (2 Tim 2:22-23)
9. He must be able to teach (2 Tim 2:24-26)

Number of pastors

The fact of the matter is that the New Testament shows us at least two pastors per church. **Period.** Many Baptists prefer one single pastor. A church can do what it wants, of course, but the apostolic model is two pastors. This cannot be denied. Again, the Bible is our guide.

The church in Jerusalem had multiple elders (Acts 11:30; 15:2, 4, 6, 22-23; 16:4; 21:18), who were (remember) distinct from the apostles. During their first missionary journey, Paul and Barnabas visited congregations of believers and "appointed **elders** for them in every church," (Acts 14:23). When Paul was on the way to Jerusalem,

---

158. "He must be faithful and skillful to declare the Mind of God, and diligent therein, also to preach in season and out of season; God having committed unto him the Ministry of Reconciliation, a most choice and sacred Trust. What Interest hath God greater in the World which he hath committed unto Men than this?" (Keach, in Dever [*Polity*, 66]).

159. Keach remarked, "He is a Steward of the Mysteries of God, therefore ought to be a Man of good Understanding and Experience, being sound in the Faith, and one that is acquainted with the Mysteries of the Gospel: Because he is to feed the People with Knowledge and Understanding," (in Dever, *Polity*, 66).

where he knew he'd be imprisoned, he "sent to Ephesus and called to him the **elders** of the church," (Acts 20:17).

In his first letter to Timothy, Paul advised him, "let the **elders** who rule well be considered worthy of double honor," (1 Tim 5:17). He also told reminded Titus that he'd left him in Crete to "amend what was defective, and appoint **elders** in every town as I directed you," (Titus 1:5). Likewise, James wrote that, if any Christian was sick, "let him call for the **elders** of the church," (Jas 5:14). And, the Apostle Peter made sure to "exhort the **elders** among you," (1 Pet 5:1) as he closed his letter with encouragement for pastors (1 Pet 5:1-10). The Apostle John considered himself an "elder," (2 John 1:1; 3 Jn 1:1).

In addition to being "**elders**," the leaders from Ephesus were also "**overseers**" (Acts 20:28). Paul wrote his letter to the Christians in the congregation at Philippi, along with "the **bishops** and deacons (Phil 1:1). Paul's comments about the desire "to the office of bishop" (1 Tim 3:1) don't mean a church should only have one of these; it just outlines the qualifications for the office (see also Titus 1:7).

In addition, the writer of Hebrews told them to "remember **your leaders**," (Heb 13:7), who he identified as those who "spoke to you the word of God." He urged these Jewish Christians to "imitate **their** faith;" that is, their leader's faith, which suggests they had multiple elders in their churches. He then warned them to "obey your **leaders** and submit to **them**; for **they** are keeping watch over your souls," (Heb 13:17). Finally, Paul told the church at Thessalonica to "respect **those** who labor among you" (1 Thess 5:12), and advised the congregation to "esteem **them** very highly," (1 Thess 5:13).

And, for the finale, Peter advised pastors, "you that are younger be subject to the **elders**," (1 Pet 5:5). He wanted the younger elders to be subject to the older ones, to learn from them and respect their age and experience. Whatever else this means, it also implies a plurality of elders in churches.

We've now surveyed *every instance* where the office of "pastor," "bishop," "elder" or "overseer" appears in the entire New Testament, or is alluded to. It's very clear it was normal for local churches to have two pastors, at least. Some Baptist theologians still argue for a single pastor model. After all, the New Testament doesn't *specifically state* a church should have two pastors, does it? For example, one theologian wrote, "To state the obvious, since the New Testament nowhere requires plural eldership, then plural eldership must not be treated as a New Testament requirement."[160]

This is a bad argument, and an inconsistent one. We're guided by the Bible, both in what it explicitly teaches and in what it shows the apostolic church doing. Regarding believers baptism, for example, we see new believers being baptized immediately. Thus, Baptists believe baptism is only for believers. Likewise, we see Jesus and the Apostle Paul affirming the Lord's Supper is for New Covenant members. Thus, we ought to allow any Christian to partake. Ironically, some Baptists refuse to allow dual pastors because the New Testament doesn't *explicitly and exactly* say so, but these same men often argue that only baptized church members can partake of the Lord's Supper based on *a series of inferences!*

The Office of the Deacon

The office of the deacon was instituted in Acts 6:1-6, and the qualifications are explained in 1 Timothy. They are as follows:

	v.8	Grave (serious or dignified)
	v.8	Not double-tongued (hypocritical)
1 Timothy 3:8-13	*v.8*	Not addicted to wine or alcohol
	v.8	Not greedy
	v.9	Lives out the Gospel ("holding the mystery of the faith") with a clear conscience
	v.10	All these requirements (above) must be tested,

---

160. Bauder (*Baptist Distinctives,* 105).

		and a man may become a deacon if he fits the requirements ("being found blameless")
	v.10	Be a man
	v.11	His wife is serious (grave, disciplined)
	v.11	His wife must not be slanderous (given to gossip or spiteful talk)
	v.11	His wife must be sober-minded
	v.11	His wife must be faithful and trustworthy in all things
	v.12	He must be a "one woman man"
	v.12	He must manage his children and his household well
Acts 6:3		Good and honest reputation
		Full of the Holy Spirit and spiritual wisdom (not a novice)

The word "deacon" is a Greek word which basically means servant or minister. So, a deacon is basically a helper and a servant for the congregation. There is nothing in the list (above) about teaching abilities. The Apostle Paul assumed the deacon would be able to manage his own household well, which implies some degree of leadership and spiritual competence.

Acts 6:1-6 is the only place where the office of the deacon is described in any detail. This passage tells us the apostles were very burdened and busy with the work of the ministry. A dispute had flared up between the Jewish Christians and the more "worldly," Hellenistic Jewish Christians in the congregation (Acts 6:1). The apostles summoned the congregation, and asked them to appoint some men from their ranks to handle "the daily distribution" to the widows (Acts 6:1), so they (the apostles) could devote their time to prayer and the teaching of the word of God (Acts 6:2-4).

Deacons help the pastors with the support needs of the church, so they can devote themselves to prayer and preaching. This is why deacons have usually been put in charge of (for example) the benevolent fund, the finances, the physical needs of the church building, helping with baptism and the Lord's Supper, helping with the material needs of the congregation, etc., etc.

Other Forms of Church Government

All this is important, because only Baptists (and some other "free church" groups) believe there are no offices beyond that of a local church pastor, and deacons. This may surprise you! Every other Christian group believes there is some kind of bureaucratic hierarchy above the local church. As we've seen from our study of the office of "apostle," that isn't the case at all. Here, I'll briefly explain the two other major forms of church government.

Episcopal government

You can think of Episcopalian government as sort of an imperial system with multiple hierarchies which all answer to one supreme authority (which could be an individual or a council). Doctrine and practice is centralized and determined by the ruling authority. Pastors are appointed by the Bishops, with little to no input from the congregation. The congregation has no say in what happens; notice that all the arrows on this little chart flow *downward.*

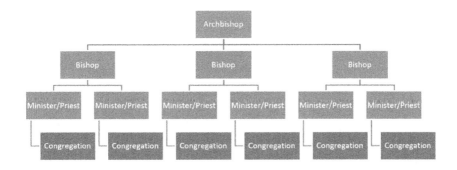

These types of churches offer some or all of the following arguments for their position:

1. apostolic succession,
2. the original authority structure of the apostles over the individual churches has continued, and
3. it's what the first churches did (e.g. James at Jerusalem)

The best example of this kind of system is the Roman Catholic Church, along with the Anglicans, the Episcopalians and the United Methodist Church. In this circumstance, if the highest authority (e.g. the Pope, in the Roman Catholic system) declared a theological position and the local church completely disagreed with that position, the local churches would be bound to obey it – period. If they refused, they would be disobedient and all sorts of consequences could result

For example, in 1950, the Roman Catholic Church officially declared the bodily assumption of Mary into heaven, without death. Pope Pius XII wrote:

> *It is forbidden to any man to change this, our declaration, pronouncement, and definition or, by rash attempt, to oppose and counter it. If any man should presume to make such an attempt, let him know that he will incur the wrath of Almighty God and of the Blessed Apostles Peter and Paul.*[161]

Also, see what the Roman Catholic Church declared at the Council of Trent about the precious doctrine of justification by faith:

> *"CANON IX.—If any one saith, that by faith alone the impious is justified, in such wise as to mean, that nothing else is*

---

161. *Apostolic Constitution of Pope Pius XII Defining the Dogma of the Assumption.* November 1, 1950. Retrieved from http://goo.gl/PexhTQ.

required to co-operate in order to the obtaining the grace of Justification, and that it is not in any way necessary, that he be prepared and disposed by the movement of his own will: let him be anathema."[162]

This is an unbiblical and illegal form of church government. The New Testament doesn't teach it. There are no officers above that of the pastors of a local church.

Presbyterian government

You can think of Presbyterianism as a sort of a representative government structure, with each lower group electing men to serve on a higher group.[163]

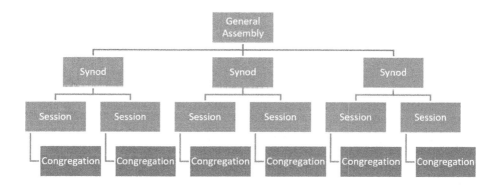

These various levels of government are comprised of a mix of Pastors and lay people. The congregation elects its own Pastors (called "elders") which, together with one or more non-Pastoral leaders in

---

162. Philip Schaff, "Council of Trent," 6th Session – On Justification – Canon IX, from *The Creeds of Christendom*, 3 vols. (New York: Harper & Brothers, 1890), 2:97.

163. The following is taken from Berkhof (*Systematic Theology*, 2:588-589). See also Reymond (*Systematic*, 901-902).

the congregation form a "Session." These people run the church, not the individual believers in the congregation.

The Sessions in a particular area elect members to serve as members of a "Presbytery." A Presbytery oversees the work of all the churches within its orbit. The Presbyteries *may* get together and elect men to serve on Synods. Likewise, they oversee the Presbyteries in their area. The highest elected body in this system is the General Assembly

This is a democracy, not a dictatorship – and each lower group elects men to constitute the higher group, and so on. This is a mix of both Pastors *and* non-Pastors – they strive for a good balance here!

However, the decisions of the higher governing bodies are final[164] There are, of course, appeals. This is *not* tyranny, because votes are taken and it was a democratic process. It is not a process where the individual church members are involved – the only thing they do is elect their own Pastors (who have to be approved by the Presbytery *before* being brought before the church for confirmation). One opponent of congregational government (the Baptist view) went so far as to say that ordinary church members are stupid sheep who need to be led![165]

This group includes Presbyterian and most Reformed churches. Therefore, again, if the General Assembly of the Presbyterian Church in the USA (a largely apostate denomination) votes to accept transgender clergy, and a local church completely disagreed with that

---

164. See especially Berkhof's view of the limitations of a local church's autonomy (*Systematic,* 2:589-590). "That the autonomy of the local church has its limitations in the relation in which it stands to the churches with which it is affiliated, and in the general interests of the affiliated churches . . . This on the one hand guards the rights and interests of the local church, but on the other hand also, the collective rights and interests of the affiliated churches. And no single church has the right to disregard matters of mutual agreement and of common interest. The local group may even be called upon occasionally to deny itself for the greater good of the Church in general," (*Systematic,* 2:590).

165. Mal Couch, *A Biblical Theology of the Church* (Grand Rapids, MI: Kregel, 1999), 166; cited by Bauder (*Baptist Distinctives,* 93).

position, then there is nothing that local church can do. All they can hope for is to lobby hard to force another vote at the next General Assembly to overturn the decision. If your local church doesn't agree with it, and you wait patiently and can't get the vote overturned at the General Assembly, your church may decide to leave the denomination. If so, it'll likely do this with no building, no ordained Pastor, no property and no money.

Congregational government

As I've already described, in the previous chapter, the congregational scheme sees pastors, deacons and the congregation mutually supporting and reinforcing one another in the life of a local church. The pastors lead with the support and consent of the congregation.

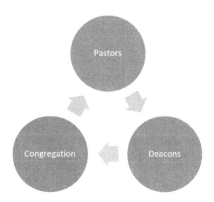

This duplicates itself in every local church, so (in theory) you should see a network and constellation of local churches cooperating for ministry, while being individually autonomous and self-governing.

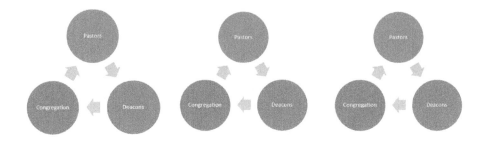

The New Testament record is clear; there are only two offices in the local church – a pastor and a deacon. There are no offices above and beyond these.

9: EACH CHRISTIAN IS A PRIEST FOR GOD

SYNOPSIS:

1. A priest's most basic job is to represent God to the people; to act as a middleman between the people and God. The Old Covenant system couldn't function without priests But now, Christ is every believer's perfect High Priest. This means priest's don't stand between God and His people anymore, because Christ is the only mediator.
2. Instead, God makes every believe an individual priest to represent Him to unbelievers and to the secular world. You're an ambassador for Christ, to show and tell Him to the culture and the people in it.
3. This means every Christian has something to contribute to the life of the congregation.

Unlike some of the other distinctives, there isn't anything uniquely "Baptist" about this mark. But, it's very, very important. Think about it; what on earth does a priest do? Think about the Old Testament. Cast your mind back to your childhood, perhaps. What is a priest's most basic job? Easy; **he represents God to the people.**

A priest is somebody who has a unique, special status before God. He's often a middleman between God and man. He offers sacrifices to God for the people, and He mediates God's Word to the people. The priest is special, because not everybody can do this work; only a priest can! In a very real way, Old Testament believers were cut off from direct, everyday access to Yahweh. Consider this, from the Old Testament:

1. A normal believer couldn't present a sacrifice to God. He had to bring it to a priest, sacrifice the animal himself, and *let the priest* apply the blood to the altar and achieve atonement for the believer's sin (see, for example, the instructions for burnt offerings in Leviticus 1; especially Leviticus 1:1-5).
2. If a believer contracted some kind of ceremonial defilement (e.g. a skin disease), the priest was responsible for imposing and lifting a quarantine (see Leviticus 13).
3. After the exile, the Israelites never had a king again. So, the priests stepped into this leadership vacuum and began acting as the spiritual leaders of the people (see, for example, Ezra 8:1-9). They were seen as uniquely appointed and trained men, who mediated God's law to the masses.
4. The High Priest was required to atone for the sins of all the people in the congregation on the Day of Atonement, "to cleanse you; from all your sins you shall be clean before the LORD," (Leviticus 16:30).

The Old Covenant kingdom could not exist without the priests. They kept the entire community in fellowship with Yahweh through the sacrificial system, atoned for all the sins of the people, maintained the ritual, ceremonial laws so the community would be "fit" to enter Yahweh's house to worship, and provided spiritual leadership. Ordinary believers couldn't do any of this.

But Jesus, the High Priest, came and changed all that. Consider what the letter to the Hebrew Christians says:

> *Since then we have a great high priest who has passed through the heavens, Jesus, the Son of God, let us hold fast our confession. For we have not a high priest who is unable to sympathize with our weaknesses, but one who in every respect has been tempted as we are, yet without sin. Let us then with confidence draw near to the throne of grace, that we may*

> *receive mercy and find grace to help in time of need (Hebrews 4:14-16).*[166]

We didn't *used* to have a great high priest, but *now* all believers have one in Christ. He's "great" because He's infinitely better than the temporary High Priests from the Old Covenant. He's the "Son of God," meaning He shares God's nature, characteristics and attributes. The Father has given Him all things, and transmitted all His glory, honor and power to Him (see Jn 5:26). Yet, He's not a cold, icy, intellectual Savior. He added a human nature to His divine nature (i.e. "took on flesh") and experienced all the awfulness of this evil world – just like you and I do!

Therefore, Jesus invites us to draw near to Yahweh's throne of grace. If you remember how things were arranged inside the tabernacle (and, later, the temples), then you know there were two compartments, and Yahweh's "throne of grace" was inside the "holy of holies," behind the veil, inside the second compartment (see 2 Chr 3:10-14).

Only the High Priest could go into the holy of holies. Yet, the letter to these Hebrew Christians invites them to march *confidently,* right through both of these figurative compartments, and *right to the very throne of grace itself*, to find mercy and help in their times of need. Jesus is the captain, prince and pioneer of our salvation (cf. Heb 2:10), and He's blazed a trail for each Christian to have direct access to Yahweh's throne. This is why that veil in the temple was torn in two when Christ died on the Cross (Mk 15:37-38).

But, what's the point? The point is that now, every single Christian is also a priest for God:

1. Christians have direct, personal access to God that unbelievers don't have

---

166. See especially the entire Book of Hebrews. A Christian would do well to ponder the whole book, and the careful argument the author made for Jesus' High Priesthood.

2. Christians represent God to a lost world
3. Christians make God known to unbelievers
4. Christians intercede before God on behalf of unbelievers

Just as an Old Covenant priest stood between God and the people, New Covenant priests do the same. But, now the audience has changed:[167]

Old Covenant Priest		New Covenant Priest
Middleman between God and God's people	vs.	Middleman between God and unbelievers

God saves Christians so that, together as a corporate group, they'd go forth to represent Him to the world. Consider what the Apostle Peter wrote (1 Peter 2:4-10):[168]

> *Because you came to Him, (the living stone who's been rejected by men, but in God's sight [is] chosen [and] precious), even you yourselves, like living stones, are being built into a spiritual house to be a holy priesthood; to offer up spiritual sacrifices, acceptable to God because of Jesus Christ.*

Christians are being built up (even now!) into a spiritual house or temple for God. Why is God doing this? So we'd be a group of holy priests, and offer up spiritual sacrifices for the Lord by the way we live our lives and serve Him. God has made *every single Christian* one of His priests.

---

167. Gregg Allision well remarked that, "Unlike the structure of the old covenant, in which a special caste of men served as priests before God and on behalf of the people of Israel, the new covenant church is composed of Christians, all of whom are considered to be priests," (*Sojourners and Strangers*, KL 7360 – 7361).

168. This quotation from 1 Peter 2, and those which follow, are from my own translation.

> This is why God says in Scripture, "Look! I have placed in Zion a stone, a cornerstone; chosen [and] precious – the one who believes in Him will never, ever be ashamed of it," (1 Peter 2:6).

The prophet Isaiah warned the corrupt Israelite leaders of His day that the time would come when He would sweep their pitiful kingdom of lies away:

> And I will make justice the line,
>   and righteousness the plummet;
> and hail will sweep away the refuge of lies,
>   and waters will overwhelm the shelter."
> Then your covenant with death will be annulled,
>   and your agreement with Sheol will not stand;
> when the overwhelming scourge passes through
>   you will be beaten down by it (Isaiah 28:17-18)

And, Isaiah promised, God would establish a lasting foundation in its place, anchored on the cornerstone of Jesus Christ, His eternal Son. Every Christian who repents and believes in the Gospel has a share in this "spiritual house" that Christ anchors.

> So, this privilege is for you -- the believers! But to those who don't believe, "the stone the builders rejected, this very one has become the head cornerstone," and "a stone to stumble on and a rock that offends them." These builders are stumbling because they're rejecting the message. Actually, they were destined for this (1 Pet 2:6-8).

Unbelievers are destined to stumble and trip over the Gospel message. That's where Christians come on the scene, to fulfill our divine mandate to be God's priests, to make the Gospel message known to the world:

> *But you believers are a chosen people, a royal priesthood, a holy nation – God's own people. The purpose of all this is so you'd announce the wonderful things God did, who called you out of the darkness [and] into His amazing light. You used to not be a people, but now you're the people of God! You weren't given any mercy, but now you've received mercy! (1 Pet 2:8-10).*

We're a chosen people, a group of royal priests who bear Yahweh's insignia on our uniform jackets. We're a holy nation of people, just as Israel was under the Old Covenant (cf. Ex 19:5-6) and will be again in the future. God made us priests so "you'd announce the wonderful things God did" in the Gospel.

So, what does all this mean? Well, there are a few key implications for Christians to consider:

1. There is no "priesthood" today, separate from the rest of God's people.

Pastors are not "super Christians" who belong to a different class. In contrast, the Roman Catholic Church believes ordination to the ministry is a "sacramental act"[169] that sets them apart and configures them to Christ in an indelible way.[170] This is heretical, and completely at odds with the Bible's teaching. Every Christian has *equal access*, *equal standing*, and *equal responsibilities* to represent Yahweh to unbelievers.

---

169. *Catechism of the Catholic Church*, Article 1554.

170. *Catechism* (Articles 1563ff).

2. "[T]here is one mediator between God and men, the man Christ Jesus," (2 Tim 2:5).

A Christian doesn't need to confess his sins to a priest and receive absolution, because Christ is the great High Priest. He's better than the priests descended from Aaron. As the letter to the Hebrew Christians said, "The former priests were many in number, because they were prevented by death from continuing in office; but he holds his priesthood permanently, because he continues for ever. Consequently he is able for all time to save those who draw near to God through him, since he always lives to make intercession for them," (Heb 7:23-25).

3. Every Christian has something to contribute to congregational life and decision-making.

This is a critical point; each Christian is competent to have a say in church life. God has made him (or her!) this way, given the gifts of the Spirit, and made each believer an individual priest. Everyone has something to contribute, and deserves to be heard.

Every Christian is a priest. If you're a Christian, because you've come to Christ you've been placed into God's spiritual house. You're an individual building-block, a LEGO-brick. You have unique gifts, talents and abilities. You have a unique personality, and God has providentially shaped and molded you into the person He wants you to be. To be sure, we all have some rough edges we need to round off, but God is shaping us, and He's placed us where He wants us.

Our job is to represent Him to the world, individually and corporately. Christ has given us direct access to God; He's in heaven right now, holding the door open to every believer to come boldly to the very throne of grace. There is no other mediator. There is no "super Christian" Pastor who stands in the gap for you. There is only Jesus Christ, the eternal Son of God, who "always lives to make intercession for [us]," (Hebrews 7:25). **Every member is equal before God, and before each other**.

> *As priests, we are not only to be consecrated to holiness by the blood, but we are to be characterized by holiness in our conduct. Perhaps these holy requirements impose a price that many are unwilling to pay, and they shun the responsibilities of the priesthood. The easy way is to look upon the preacher as the responsible party. It is his job to be holy; it is his job to pray and offer sacrifices. But this is not God's way.*[171]

Or, as this guy says:

---

171. Paul R. Jackson, *The Doctrine and Administration of the Church,* 3rd ed. (Schaumburg: Regular Baptist Press, 2014), 143 – 144. Emphasis added.

10: EVERY PERSON HAS FREEDOM OF CONSCIENCE

> **SYNOPSIS:**
>
> 1. People are personally responsible for what they believe; God judges people individually.
> 2. Jesus and the apostles preached individual responsibility.
> 3. Faith can't be compelled, coerced or manipulated out of somebody. God has His people, and He's calling them from every tribe, tongue, people and nation in the world. Only His Spirit changes hearts and minds.
> 4. This means government should leave believers of all faiths alone to worship (or not) as they see fit.

Can you force somebody to become a Christian? Can you force a Christian to see things your way on, say, infant baptism? Baptists have always read the Bible and seen that a man is responsible to God for his own sin – period. You can persuade, you can explain, you can even beg if you want to. But, you can't point a gun at a man and "make" him a Christian. You also can't persecute him and threaten him to become the same "type" of Christian you are, either. As one Baptist theologian put it, "to be responsible, man must be free."[172]

Why? Because each person ultimately has to answer to God for himself. Nobody can hide behind the state or the Pastor and say, "It's not my fault! He *told* me what to believe!"

---

172. E. Y. Mullins, *The Axioms of Religion* (Philadelphia: American Baptist Publication Society, 1908; reprint; Watertown: Roger Williams Heritage Archives, 2003), 74.

This might not seem like a Baptist distinctive, but it is. Baptists, and some other groups, are sometimes called "free church" movements because, well ... we think the church should be "free" from external control. This distinctive of personal responsibility for what you believe is the *individual* application of the free church principle.

Throughout Scripture, God holds people individually responsible for what they believe. True faith can't be coerced or compelled; it has to be voluntary.

- Adam and Eve made a choice to believe God's promise of a future heir, who would destroy Satan one day.
- Cain made a choice to murder his brother. No doubt, he conformed to his parent's wishes in an external way while he was younger. But, when he came of age, he went his own way.
- Noah made a choice to believe God, and remain faithful. The others, who drowned in the flood, made their choices, too.

And so it goes. Real repentance and faith can't be compelled; it must come from the heart. So, this distinctive has at least two implications:

1. Government should leave believers *of all faiths* alone to worship (or not) as they see fit.

Religion is not a "state" matter; it's a private affair between a man and God (however he may conceive of Him). This means Baptists in America shouldn't be happy when a local government prevents a mosque from being built. What if the tables were turned, and Baptists were forbidden from starting a new church in an urban center? What then? Everyone deserves freedom of conscience; this is a universal human right.[173]

2. People are personally responsible for what they believe.

This means winsome and prayerful persuasion are the order of the day. Compulsion, manipulation and coercion are meaningless tools, and any Christian who uses them ought to be ashamed.

One Baptist historian remarked that these distinctions "reshaped the modern world. They add up to what is presently called religious liberty and separation of church and state."[174] To truly appreciate these timeless truths, you have to understand the context they arose from.

Baptist Beginnings

The Baptist "identity" emerged during persecution in 17th century England. Queen Mary (1553 – 1558) had restored Roman Catholicism to England after Protestantism's progress during her father's reign. Mary's sister and successor, Elizabeth I, sought to find a middle way; to thread the needle between both the Roman Catholic and Protestant factions.[175] This attempt at a *via media* is why some Christians mistakenly believe the Church of England was not greatly impacted by the Protestant Reformation. It's also why, on a popular level, the late comedian Robin Williams once jokingly referred to the

---

173. For more on this, see especially Os Guinness, *The Global Public Square: Religious Freedom and the Making of a World Safe for Diversity* (Downers Grove. Zondervan, 2013).

174. McBeth (*Baptist Heritage*, 102).

175. For context, see especially Beale, *Baptist History*, chapter 2.

Episcopal Church (that is, the member of the Anglican Communion based in the United States) as "Catholic-lite."

After Elizabeth assumed the throne, Parliament quickly passed the Act of Uniformity (1558), which ordered the following:[176]

1. All churches must use the *Book of Common Prayer*[177] "in such order and form as is mentioned in the said book" for all services.
2. Any minister who did not follow the *Book of Common Prayer's* prescribed pattern for any church function, or who spoke "anything in the derogation or depraving of the said book, or anything therein contained, or of any part thereof," would lose all ministry pay for one year, and be imprisoned for six months. If a minister offended a second time, and was convicted, he would be imprisoned for an entire year.
3. Any person who was "depraving, or despising of the same book, or of anything therein contained, or any part thereof, or shall, by open fact, deed, or by open threatenings, compel or cause" a minister to do the same would be fined.
4. Weekly, every citizen must "diligently and faithfully, having no lawful or reasonable excuse to be absent, endeavour themselves to resort to their parish church or chapel ..." or be fined.

---

176. All excerpts to the Act of Uniformity are from an online version published by Hanover College, located at https://history.hanover.edu/texts/engref/er80.html.

177. The *Book of Common Prayer* (1549) was the creation of Thomas Cranmer, the Archbishop of Canterbury. It met a genuine need by prescribing orders of service and liturgy for all events in the cycle of church life. It will be difficult for the reader to appreciate the Act of Uniformity's insistence on the *Book of Common Prayer* if he isn't familiar with its contents.

The Anglican Communion, and its various branches, have updated the *Book of Common Prayer* many times, but its essential nature remains the same. You can view the Church of England's current edition of the *Book of Common Prayer* online at https://www.churchofengland.org/prayer-and-worship/worship-texts-and-resources/book-common-prayer.

Given this climate, "[a]nyone in London who tried to promote the notion of independent, congregational churches ran the danger of imprisonment and public execution. It was from the establishment of Elizabeth's Act of Uniformity that many Puritans acquired the label *nonconformists*."[178]

Elizabeth passed away after 45 years on the throne, and James VI of Scotland (later, James I of England) took her place. Various religious groups, among them Separatists, Roman Catholics and Presbyterians, all tried to court favor with the new sovereign, King James I (yes, the "KJV" King James). Separatists were sadly mistaken if they felt they had a friend in King James.

One Baptist theologian, Leon McBeth, observed "[t]he idea of religious liberty horrified him."[179] James, that "most dread sovereign" whom God sent by "great and manifold" blessings[180] to rule over England, was determined to exercise authority over the church as well as the state. He believed it was "the chiefest of kingly duties . . . to settle affairs of religion."[181]

The separatists, however, couldn't disagree more. They urged King James I to show mercy. "They asserted that every man had a right to judge for himself in matters of religion and that to persecute on account of religion is illegal and antichristian."[182] James I feared a freedom of conscience in religion might well lead to civil anarchy. He saw a very basic political necessity for religious conformity; a sentiment shared by his son, Charles I. It was therefore the policy of

---

178. Beale, *Baptist History*, 27.

179. McBeth (*Baptist Heritage*, 100).

180. From the "Epistle Dedicatory" to the King James Bible.

181. McBeth, *Baptist Heritage,* 100.

182. John T. Christian, *A History of the Baptists,* 2 vols. (Texarkana: Bogard Press, 1922; Kindle reprint, 2013), vol. 1, Kindle Locations 4109-4110.

the Crown to harass and persecute dissenters from the Church of England. Baptist identity in Britain was forged in the midst of this persecution.

One early Baptist (perhaps the first official "Baptist"), John Smythe (1612) stated, in embryo form, the very principles of religious liberty many Baptists continue to argue for today. Essentially, he asserted that Baptists recognized the civil authority of the state, but "would not allow the government to determine or regulate their relation to God."[183]

> *That the magistrate is not by virtue of his office to meddle with religion, or matters of conscience, to force or compel men to this or that form of religion, or doctrine: but to leave Christian religion free, to every man's conscience, and to handle only civil transgressions (Rom xiii), injuries and wrongs of man against man, in murder, adultery, theft, etc., for Christ only is the king, and lawgiver of the church and conscience (James iv. 12).*[184]

Other Baptists, such as Thomas Helwys (1612), plainly stated that any man should be free to worship, or not, as he pleased without *any* interference from the state.[185]

> *And we bow ourselves to the earth . . . beseeching the King to judge righteous judgment herein, whether there be so unjust a thing, and of so great cruel tyranny, under the sun, as to force men's consciences in their religion to God, seeing that if they*

---

183. McBeth, *Baptist Heritage*, 102.

184. John Smyth, "On Religious Liberty," from H. Leon McBeth, *A Sourcebook for Baptist Heritage* (Nashville: B&H, 1990), 70.

185. McBeth, *Baptist Heritage*, 103.

> err, they must pay the price of their transgression with the loss of their souls.
>
> Oh, let the King judge, is it not most equal that men should chose their religion themselves, seeing they must only stand themselves before the judgment seat of God to answer for themselves, when it shall be no cause for them to say, 'we were commanded or compelled to be of this religion' by the King, or by them that had authority from him . . .[186]

He also wrote this:

> For men's religion to God, is between God and themselves; the King shall not answer for it, neither may the King be judge between God and man. Let them be heretics, Turks, Jews, or whatsoever; it appertains not to the earthly power to punish them in the least measure.[187]

Leonard Busher (1614) colorfully, but somewhat crassly, compared forced worship to spiritual rape. Busher argued that "regeneration is the result of faith in Christ; and that no king or bishop is able to command faith. Persecution, therefore, is irrational, and must fail of its object; men cannot be made Christians by force."[188] He wrote:

> . . . to constrain princes and peoples to receive that one true religion of the gospel, is wholly against the mind and merciful

---

186. Thomas Helwys, "The Mistery of Iniquity," from McBeth, *Sourcebook*, 72. I modernized the spelling.

187. Ibid.

188. Christian, *History of the Baptists,* vol. 1, KL 4138-4139.

> *law of Christ, dangerous both to king and state, a means to decrease the kingdom of Christ, and a means to increase the kingdom of antichrist . . .*[189]

Also, this:

> *And no king nor bishop can, or is able to command faith; That is the gift of God, who worketh in us both the will and the deed of his own good pleasure. Set him not a day, therefore, in which, if his creature hear not and believe not, you will imprison and burn him.*
>
> *Paul was a blasphemer and also a persecutor, and could not be converted by the apostles and ministers of Christ; yet at last was received to mercy, and converted extraordinarily by Christ himself . . . And as kings and bishops cannot command the wind, so they cannot command faith; . . . You may force men to church against their consciences, but they will believe as they did afore.*[190]

Baptists stood on the Scriptures when they declared that men must never have their religious convictions forced. The Baptists, and other dissenters, had a brief respite during the time of Oliver Cromwell, but that all came crashing down when the monarchy was restored and the Church of England was welcomed back as the official state church. Armitage writes that "the Baptists became, as usual, the special subjects of hate, storm and chains; prisons and doom became their gloomy fate."[191]

---

189. Leonard Busher, "Religion's Peace, 1614," from McBeth, *Sourcebook*, 73.

190. Ibid.

191. Thomas Armitage, *A History of the Baptists* (New York: Bryan, Taylor & Co., 1890; reprint, Watertown: Roger Williams Archive, n.d.), 603.

The updated Act of Uniformity (1662) decreed that all ministers "declare ... unfeigned assent and consent to all and everything contained and prescribed in and by the Book entitled 'The Book of Common Prayer and Administration of the Sacraments and other Rites and Ceremonies of the Church,' according to the use of the Church of England."[192]

The Conventicle Act (1664) forbade unauthorized worship services with more than five persons present, aged 16 or up, beyond the immediate family.[193] The Act was passed to guard "against the growing and dangerous practices of seditious sectaries and other disloyal persons who, under pretense of tender consciences, do at their meetings contrive insurrections ..."[194] People who were convicted of this "crime" were imprisoned for up to 90 days, but could be released early if they paid a fine.

Another act even forbade ejected ministers from forming new congregations within five miles of their previous residence.

King Charles II *did* declare a year-long moratorium on persecution, provided dissenters register to receive leniency. When the tide of public opinion shifted one year later, these same registers were used to hunt down dissenters![195] Desperate Baptists resorted to all manner

---

192. This excerpt is from the text of the 1662 Act of Uniformity, posted online by the University of London at https://www.british-history.ac.uk/statutes-realm/vol5/pp364-370#h3-0015.

193. The Act explained that any such gatherings "under colour or pretence of any Exercise of Religion in other manner then is allowed by the Liturgy or practise of the Church of England" were illegal. This excerpt is from the text of the 1664 Conventicle Act, posted online by the University of London at https://www.british-history.ac.uk/statutes-realm/vol5/pp516-520#h2-0001.

194. This excerpt is from the text of the 1664 Conventicle Act, posted online by the University of London at https://www.british-history.ac.uk/statutes-realm/vol5/pp516-520#h2-0001. Spelling was modernized.

195. McBeth, *Baptist Heritage,* 115-116.

of deception and ingenuity in order to simply meet for worship. One desperate plea to the King sums up the Baptist experience in this time of tribulation:

> *We dare not walk the streets, and are abused even in our own houses. If we pray to God with our families, we are threatened to be hung. Some of us are stoned almost to death, and others imprisoned for worshiping God according to the dictates of our consciences and the rule of his word.*[196]

What's the Point?

Here's the takeaway:

1. God judges people individually.

See, for example 1 Corinthians 3:11-15, where Paul discusses how believer's works for the Lord will be judged, in the end. Also consider the terrible scene from Jesus' "great white throne," where unbelievers will be judged on the last day (Rev 20:11-15). And, the Apostle Peter reminds us that the Father "judges each one impartially according to his deeds," (1 Pet 1:17).

2. Jesus preached individual responsibility.

He told the crowd to "repent, and believe the Gospel!" (Mk 1:15). He "came not to call the righteous, but sinners," (Mk 2:17). He taught the disciples to do the same thing, "so they went out and preached that men should repent," (Mk 6:12). Even Jesus' enemies, the Jewish leaders, understood He wanted them to individually believe in His message (Mk 15:31-32).

---

196. Armitage, *History of the Baptists,* 603.

3. The Apostles preached personal responsibility.

The apostolic sermons (see Acts 2 – 4, 13, etc.) are full of appeals to repent and believe the Gospel.

All this is why Baptists believe so passionately in freedom of conscience, and personal responsibility in matters of religion. This puts the onus for acceptance or rejection of the Gospel on the individual. Faith can't be compelled, coerced or manipulated out of somebody. God has His people, and He's calling them from every tribe, tongue, people and nation in the world. His Spirit changes hearts and minds; He does what threats, guns, knives and machetes can't. He gives spiritual life, which only comes by hearing the Gospel of Jesus Christ preached and explained.

As Baptist historian Thomas Armitage explained,[197]

> *We may regret that all men are not Christians, and wish that they were, and we may wish that they held Christian principles as we hold them, but we have no right to enforce our doctrines by law, and others have no right to force their doctrines upon us by human statute.*
>
> *We hold that if a man chooses to be a Mohammedan, a Jew, a Pagan, a Roman Catholic, a Protestant or an Infidel, he has a right to be that, so far as the civil law is concerned. Therefore, all persecution for the maintenance of this or that religion is radically wrong …*

---

197. Thomas Armitage, "Baptist Faith and Practice," in *Baptist Doctrines,* ed. C.A. Jenkens (St. Louis: C.R. Barns, 1890; reprint; Watertown: Roger Williams Heritage Archive, 2003), 36-37. Emphasis mine.

When a Baptist shall rob one man of soul-liberty, by statute, penalty and sword, he will cease to be a Baptist for that reason.

11: CONCLUSION – why you should care, and how churches can begin fixing things

Being a Baptist matters. It's a shorthand for a whole host of doctrines which explain how we believe the Lord wants his local churches to operate. Only the New Testament tells us how to "do church."

1. If we look to the Old Covenant for how to "do church," then Baptists believe you're doing it wrong. The New Covenant is, well ... *new,* and it has a new structure and organization.
2. If church members don't *have* to be confessing, believing Christians, then little children may grow up believing they're believers just because they were baptized as babies. They'll make the same mistake the Israelites did, with their two-tiered Covenant. Some may never make the deliberate leap to the second-tier, and die believing they're one of God's children. The New Covenant is only for confessing believers, and the official membership of the New Covenant community (i.e. the church) is, too.
3. Baptists believe the ordinance of baptism symbolizes the beauty of the New Covenant in a variety of ways, including a divine washing from our sins by the Spirit, and identification with the death, burial and resurrection of Jesus Christ.
4. Baptists believe the Lord's Supper is a memorial; a vehicle for renewal in Christ as we remember His broken body, His shed

blood, and His promise to return one day to set everything right.
5. Churches are separate from the state, and ought to be left alone to govern themselves. The only "state" which should govern Christ's church is Christ Himself, when He establishes His Father's kingdom.
6. The only church officers are pastors and deacons, and there is no bureaucratic hierarchy (or mandated church office) beyond these offices in a local church.
7. Each Christian is a priest for God, has equal standing before the Lord, and enjoys direct and personal access to the throne of grace.
8. Every person has freedom of conscience, and coercion, manipulation and compulsion regarding matters of faith (or no faith) are shameful injustices. This means government should never favor or legislate for one religion over the other, and everyone is personally responsible to God for what he believes, and why.

What Should We Do?

Christians in Baptist churches need to know the name on their church matters. It doesn't give them any style points, and I know the name "First Baptist Church" isn't as "woke" as "LifePointe." But, let's be honest – vague and generic church names often don't communicate much. The name "Baptist" *does* communicate, and no Christian should ever be ashamed of this heritage.

There are several things Baptists can begin doing to help people understand why this name, and everything it represents, matters. None of them are easy, and they each presuppose a commitment to thorough, substantive and sound teaching of Scripture:

Pastors should regularly teach and preach the distinction between the Old and New Covenants.

It's baffling to me how Christians can attend church their entire lives, and not be able to explain the difference between the Old and New Covenants, or why it matters. There are many reasons for this. If you attend a dispensationalist church, your Pastor might have been trained to believe the New Covenant has nothing to do with the church. Also, many dispensationalists are trained to see the dispensations, not the biblical covenants, as the framework to understand the biblical storyline.

And, finally, because Baptists believe so firmly in local church autonomy, each Baptist pastor has been selected and ordained by an *individual church*. This means the onus for quality control is on the local church, not a higher bureaucratic body. The result is a very uneven quality of professional ministers. Most Baptist pastors do not hold a Master of Divinity degree, and have received little to no graduate training.

Be that as it may, this is no excuse. The distinction between the Old and New Covenants is so fundamental to a right understanding of the Bible, and the Bible's storyline, that it's inexcusable to not make this a regular part of a congregation's teaching and preaching ministries. If church members don't understand this distinction, and the blessed benefits of this new and better covenant built upon better promises, then they'll never appreciate why regenerate church membership is the defining mark of Baptist identity.

Pastors should teach periodic courses on comparative denominations, and focus particular attention on church membership, infant baptism, and the membership of the New Covenant.

Church leaders can do this in a number of ways. A Pastor can invite a friendly, irenic Presbyterian minister to address his Sunday School class. Ask him to explain (a) why he baptizes infants, (b) why he sees a two-tiered continuity between the Old and New Covenants, (c) why he thinks Baptists are wrong to *not* baptize infants, and (d) who a church member is. A leader can prep the church before the visit about what to expect, and allow generous time for questions and answers after the Presbyterian brother speaks.

A Pastor can also show the congregation a video of a gracious, professional debate between a knowledgeable Baptist and a knowledgeable Presbyterian. He can stop and start the debate, and discuss the points of view along the way. For starters, I'd suggest an excellent discussion between James White (Reformed Baptist) and Gregg Strawbridge (Presbyterian) from 2015 (see the footnote for the link).[198] Another good option is a debate between James White and Bill Shishko, which can also be watched on YouTube.[199]

In short, Pastors should make a real effort to explain why Baptists are different, and why these differences matter. This shouldn't be done in a malicious, nasty sort of way, as if non-Baptists aren't Christians. This is an inter-family dispute, but it's a disagreement that matters.

Pastors should make a dedicated, concerted effort to make believer's baptism meaningful in the life of the church.

Pastors should preach sermons about what believer's baptism is, and what the New Testament has to say about it on a periodic basis. Not the *same sermon* over and over, but different ones. It's a fact that the New Testament knows nothing of an unbaptized Christian.

---

198. Alpha and Omega Ministries, "The Baptism Debate James White vs Gregg Strawbridge," published June 23, 2015. Retrieved from YouTube at: https://bit.ly/2Jbx8Rf.

199. Alpha and Omega Ministries, "The Baptism Debate," published March 10 2014. Retrieved from YouTube at: https://bit.ly/2GNFu39.

Candidates should provide a credible and substantive explanation of their conversion, and be able to accurately explain what the ordinance symbolizes and pictures. Believer's baptism is a public confession of a newfound faith. This might mean little children should wait to be baptized until they can explain what it means, and what their salvation consists of. "Seeing young children nod assent to a pastor's question may be very precious or cute to parents, but it is not an adequate symbol of commitment."[200]

During baptism itself, the candidate can give his profession while standing in the baptistry and make a commitment to the congregation and to the Lord.

Below, I've provided an example of what this can look like. These questions can be addressed to the candidate as he stands in the baptistry, wearing baptismal robes, facing the congregation. Also, in this example, I'm assuming the candidate is a new believer who has already been "voted in" by the congregation, and will become a member of the congregation immediately after baptism:

Questions about Baptism

1. Why does God command Christians to be baptized?
2. Is baptism for believers or unbelievers?
3. Are you a believer?
4. Have you repented of your sins, and believed in who Jesus Christ is and what He's done?
5. Please explain how the Lord saved you.
6. During baptism, going under the water is a picture of Jesus' burial. What does this represent what God has done for you?
7. During baptism, coming up out of the water is a picture of Jesus' resurrection. What does this represent God has done for you?
8. *The pastor reads Romans 6:4.* Your physical baptism in water is a picture of what Christ has done to your soul – your old person is buried and gone, and you've been born again and been given new life. What does the Apostle Paul mean when he says, "we were buried therefore with him by baptism into death, so that as Christ

---

200. Hammett (*Biblical Foundations,* 276).

> was raised from the dead by the glory of the Father, we too might walk in newness of life,"?
> 9. The Apostle Paul said that, when you repent and believe the Gospel, "he saved us, not because of deeds done by us in righteousness, but in virtue of his own mercy, by the washing of regeneration and renewal in the Holy Spirit, which he poured out upon us richly through Jesus Christ our Savior, so that we might be justified by his grace and become heirs in hope of eternal life," (Titus 3:5-7). What does the water of baptism represent that God has done or you?
>
> **Questions about Covenant Membership in a Local Church**
>
> 1. Do you promise before God Almighty and your Savior Jesus Christ to do your best to serve God every day because you love Him and want to prove your love by action?
> 2. Do you agree to worship and serve the Lord as best you can in this congregation, as brothers and sisters in the body of Christ?
> 3. Do you swear to love the members of this congregation as brothers and sisters in Christ?
> 4. Do you promise to be always trying to grow in your knowledge of God, your personal holiness, and your love for Him?
> 5. Do you promise to regularly read God's Holy Word so you know how God wants you to live, so you can be convicted of your own sin, and so you can be encouraged to grow closer to Him, and be more Christ-like day by day?
> 6. Do you promise to be a public testimony for Jesus Christ by living a Godly life, and telling the Gospel message to others?
> 7. Do you pledge to remember your fellow church members in prayer?
> 8. Do you pledge to be willing to learn from other church members, and even be corrected by them, if necessary?
> 9. Do you promise to be a faithful and active slave for Jesus Christ, among the people in this congregation, as long as you're able, or until God calls you elsewhere?

Pastors should make a dedicated effort to make the Lord's Supper a meaningful event for growth and sanctification in the local church.

The Lord's Supper has fallen on hard times in Baptist churches.

Few pastors preach on the topic. Fewer remind the congregation when it's being observed, so they have little or no opportunity to prepare themselves through self-examination and repentance. When the Supper is observed, it's often tacked on to the end of a sermon as an afterthought.

There is often little to no warning or call or introspection given (see my example, above, about one way to do this well). And, it's often conducted in a lazy way, so that the congregation is rarely reminded about what the ordinance symbolizes and pictures. It becomes something to "get over with" before lunch, not a true means of growth.

I suggest pastors formulate several "orders of service" to celebrate the Lord's Supper, to make the ordinance meaningful in church life.

Pastors' should make a deliberate effort to ensure "new believers" are *actually believers*, before allowing them to officially join the congregation. This will make membership actually mean something.

It would be very prudent to withhold believer's baptism until the pastors can confirm the person is actually a believer. This doesn't need to be a *long* period of time. But, it should be long enough to do a short bible study about understanding salvation[201] and to do a systematic study of the local church's doctrinal statement. Combined, these two steps could constitute a "new membership" class. "It is far better to know and reject the gospel, then to be baptized and think one is safe without ever coming to an understanding of the gospel or what it

---

201. I suggest something like the study booklet by James Dyet, *Understanding Salvation* (Arlington Heights: Regular Baptist Press, 2005). This is an excellent tool. In fact, the entire first set of the BUILD-UP series from Regular Baptist Press is a ready-made discipleship toolkit for new believers. The pastors or deacons, or a woman teacher (if appropriate) can go through these bible studies with new believers.

means to place saving faith in Christ."[202]

Should churches not baptize very little children? The Bible doesn't say, one way or the other. The key is to make sure the candidate actually understands salvation and the significance of believer's baptism. Some churches have an official policy that they won't baptize anyone under 12, for example. Others have no such policy, believing every child is different.

My person preference would be to wait until they're 12. I've baptized younger children, and had grave doubts about whether they *truly* understood what was happening. Sure, they repeated the right words and answered all the right questions. But, I'm not sure they really understood. The better the candidate understands the Gospel, the more meaningful believer's baptism and church membership both become to them and the congregation that witnesses the events.

Pastors should commit to practicing redemptive church discipline.

The classic passage on church discipline is 1 Corinthians 5. I won't discuss that chapter in great detail, but I'll say enough to show how important redemptive church discipline is. This chapter is a template for how to handle public, scandalous sins that impact the entire congregation and the unbelieving community it ministers to.

Paul wrote that, "it is actually reported that there is immorality among you, and of a kind that is not found even among pagans; for a man is living with his father's wife," (1 Cor 5:1). We can learn four things about this situation.

First, the sin is public knowledge. It's been "reported" to Paul, and he's not even there. This means *everybody* knows about it. This is not a private sin that effects one or two people; this is a public sin that's *common knowledge* throughout the entire congregation. We know this, because somebody wrote to Paul and told him all about it. More

---

202. Hammett (*Biblical Foundations,* 122).

than that, it's also likely a sin that is known *outside* the walls of the church – it can't be contained, it's public knowledge!

In short, this particular sin has reached the point where it has become a scandal. Everybody *inside* the church knows about it. People *outside* the church know about it, and are probably whispering, gossiping and laughing about the congregation behind their backs.

Second, the sin was on-going and unrepentant. The Bible tells us to forgive *repentant* sinners. Repentance means to confess and forsake your sin. Talk by itself is cheap and meaningless; where are the "fruit that befits repentance?" (Mt 3:8). This sin is ongoing ("there *is* immorality"), which means the sinner *is still sinning* as Paul wrote this very letter, and the church hasn't done anything about it. The "report" from the congregation is also present-tense. So, the scandal is not going away; in fact, it grows ever worse with each passing *day, week, month* and *moment* that it is tolerated.

Third, the sinner claims to be a Christian. This sin happened "among you," meaning the unrepentant sinner is a member of this church at Corinth. He has a profession of faith, he has shown fruit of salvation in the past, and yet he's involved in public, scandalous, unrepentant, deliberate and continual sin! There's clearly a problem in paradise.

Fourth, the sin is universally known to be evil. The specific situation here is incest; sexual immorality with his mother-in-law. The larger point is that the sin is so obvious, so common-sense, so plain and so crystal-clear that *even unbelievers* know it's sinful, and they're not even Christians!

Again, this situation in Corinth is a template for God's people, to tell us how to handle this kind of situation – and here is the situation:

- You have a professing Christian and a church member
- The church member is engaging in obvious, blatant, clear and plain actions which even unbelievers would acknowledge is sinful

- This sin is public; it's known by people inside the church and outside – it's become a local scandal
- The church member is continuing the sin and is unrepentant about it

There is no need for hand-wringing, head-shaking, ho-humming, tap-dancing or fence-straddling. There is only one single question – do churches care about what God's word says, or not? One theologian made this remark, and it's applicable in this situation:

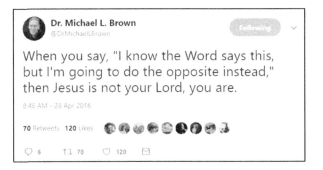

Paul tells the church at Corinth to expel the man from the church, to excommunicate him ("you are to deliver this man to Satan," 1 Cor 5:5). Why should they do this? So the sinning Christian will be driven to see the seriousness of his actions; he'll hopefully have some sense shocked into him and begin to put to death those wicked lusts ("for the destruction of the flesh," (1 Cor 5:5), so he can be sure his spirit "may be saved in the day of the Lord Jesus," (1 Cor 5:5).

This sinner pollutes the congregation, like a cancerous virus. The Corinthians must purge him out; "do you not know that a little leaven leavens the whole lump? Cleanse out the old leaven that you may be a new lump," (1 Cor 5:6-7). The church members shouldn't even associate with a professing Christian who lives a deliberately and unrepentant immoral life (1 Cor 5:9-11). In fact, Paul specifically tells them they *must judge* among themselves, and maintain holy behavior:

> *Is it not those inside the church whom you are to judge? God judges those outside. "Drive out the wicked person from among you," (1 Cor 5:12-13).*

If a church wants to make membership meaningful, wants to make personal holiness meaningful, and wants to take the Bible seriously, it must begin practicing redemptive church discipline. To be sure, that doesn't mean a Pharisaical, self-righteous inquisition of pastors and deacons. It *does* mean the church members should hold members accountable for living holy Christian lives. And, when all lesser means have failed (and believe me, there are *plenty* of lesser means), then redemptive discipline must be an option.

What's in a Name?

Ours is a proud and noble heritage. We believe it's the way God wants His church to run. We shouldn't be ashamed of our name. We should teach it, explain it, and make our people proud to wear the name "Baptist." It stands for something. It stands for God's way of doing church.

APPENDIX 1 - THE CHRISTIAN AND GOVERNMENT

What is a Christian's responsibility to secular government? What is a local church's responsibility? A lot has been written on this, and not all of it is helpful. The Apostle Peter can help us out, here (1 Pet 2:13-17):[203]

> *Submit yourselves to every human authority because of the Lord, whether to [the] emperor as one who governs, or to [the] officials who are being sent by him to punish evildoers and praise those who do right. Because this is God's will, that by doing right you'd silence the ignorant slander of foolish men -- like freed slaves, and not like those who're wearing this freedom like a cloak of wickedness, but like God's slaves.*
>
> *Respect all men. Love the family of believers. Always have fearful reverence for God. Always respect the Emperor.*

What are Christians supposed to submit to? Some translations say "ordinances of men" (e.g. KJV, NKJV), which gives the idea that we have to submit to *laws*. Other translations read "every human institution" (e.g. RSV, ESV, NASB), and that could mean a lot of different things! And, some translations say, "every human authority" (e.g. NIV), which seems to specify government officials. So, what is it? Who is it?

The true sense seems to be the offices of authority, particularly the *people* who hold these offices. Peter goes on to give examples of

---

203. This is my own translation.

the emperor and his subordinate officials. Peter says a Christian must submit to government officials and the offices they hold, at all levels. By extension, a Christian needs to obey the officials *and* the laws and ordinances they pass.

In Peter's day, the officials in question could have been temple guards, the Israelite High Priest, a member of the Sanhedrin, a Roman government official, the Roman emperor and all kinds of civil officials in various cities.

In our day, we're talking about police, fire, emergency services personnel, civil servants (i.e. bureaucrats) in local, state and federal government, regulatory agencies in local, state and federal government, elected officials in local, state and federal government, the President of the United States, your parents, the judicial courts, supervisors at work, etc.

These isn't an easy command to follow, especially when you consider some of the bureaucrats in local, state and federal government, or some of the elected officials today! Some disciples thought Jesus advocated armed resistance at the Last Supper (Lk 22:35-38), and some even asked if they should "strike with the sword" when the temple officers came to arrest Jesus in the Garden of Gethsemane (Lk 22:47-51).

They were wrong; Jesus *did not* advocate armed resistance to civil authorities. See, for example, His answer to the chief priest's spies about whether a man ought to pay taxes to the Roman government (Luke 20:19-26),[204] and their later lie to Pilate at His trial (Luke 23:2).

When Herod Agrippa arrested Peter (Acts 12:1-3), the Christians in Jerusalem *didn't mount a rescue attempt*; instead, they prayed (Acts 12:5). When Paul was arrested by civil authorities during his missionary travels (e.g. Acts 16:19-24), we have no indication he ever

---

204. Briefly, their motivation was to entice Jesus to admit that, because He was the "Messiah" (though they obviously didn't accept this claim), His kingdom had to be given priority and, thus, Jewish people were no longer obligated to pay taxes to a pagan government. This plot failed, obviously. Jesus' kingdom reign has not yet begun.

fought back. In fact, he demanded they apologize for their error in discharging their office (Acts 16:35-40).

But, how should Peter's command shape how Christians refer to these people (the "human authorities") and treat them in our public and inter-personal discourse (e.g. conversations with friends, family, social media, etc.)? After all, Peter isn't just talking about pouty, unwilling submission to civil authority. He isn't saying Christians should do what government officials say, no matter what it is, because they say so. He's also referring to attitude, mindset, mentality and a demeanor we should have that describes *how* we submit to civil authorities when we interact with them.

Whenever we refer to or interact with government officials, whether they're elected or civil service, local, state or federal officials, emergency services personnel or bureaucrats, we need to do so with gentleness, Christlike character and respect. This *especially includes* our interactions on social media and in personal conversations.

In short, whether we personally agree or disagree with the person holding the office, we should always act like Christian ladies and gentlemen and "submit ourselves," insofar as we can. Remember that Paul immediately apologized when he inadvertently insulted the Israelite High Priest (Acts 23:1-5). He didn't respect the man, but he respected the office.

This isn't the way our culture operates today. Our culture encourages people to act petulant, childish, angry and crazed when they don't like a politician or agree with his politics or policies. For example, in August 2017, a white supremacist deliberately drove his vehicle into a crowd during a rally in Charlottesville, NC. One woman was killed and 19 others were injured.[205]

---

205. For background, see Joe Heim, "Recounting a day of rage, hate, violence and death," *Washington Post* (August 14, 2017).

President Donald Trump tweeted his condolences, which isn't an unusual thing for a President to do:[206]

The Washington State Governor, Jay Inslee, tweeted a rebuke to President Trump about his comments:[207]

Several people responded. Among them were this man:[208]

---

206. This tweet can be found at
    https://twitter.com/realDonaldTrump/status/896512981319790592.

207. This tweet can be found at:
    https://twitter.com/GovInslee/status/896463491539718144.

208. This tweet can be found at:
    https://twitter.com/roast_chuck/status/897517232242081792.

and this man:[209]

There's nothing particularly *nasty* about these exchanges; they're typical of what you find on social media today. But, is this how Christians should respond to government officials? Does this reflect the kind of heart the Apostle Peter commands us to have? Christians can be just as snarky on social media about politicians, bureaucrats and elected officials as anyone else, *but should we be?*

---

209. This tweet can be found at:
   https://twitter.com/SciCommic/status/896468627313934336.

Below, we see President Trump tweet support to the State of Texas in the aftermath of Hurricane Harvey in 2017:[210]

This man, who identifies as a Christian minister, replied:[211]

---

210. This tweet can be found at:
https://twitter.com/realDonaldTrump/status/904025340049285121.

211. This tweet can be found at:
https://twitter.com/TalbertSwan/status/904059982039072769.

193

In another incident, President Trump revoked the Golden State Warrior's invite to the White House in 2017:[212]

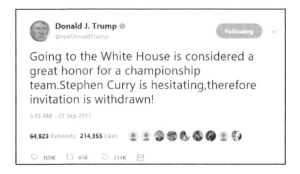

and NBA basketball star LeBron James replied:[213]

These examples might seem trivial. After all, we have no idea if these people are Christians. Why should you care? You should care because this kind of attitude is representative of the mindset Christians can so easily slip into when commenting on social media, and even in private conversations. When it comes to a local church's relationship with a secular government, we shouldn't only think in

---

212. President Trump's tweet can be found here:
https://twitter.com/realDonaldTrump/status/911572182060453893.

213. The tweet can be found here:
https://twitter.com/KingJames/status/911610455877021697.

terms of "big events," like Peter and John before the Jewish authorities (Acts 4). For most of us, the practical outworking of this command comes in how we speak about and interact with government officials and their laws, day in and day out, in small ways.

As Christians, we can do better and we must do better. Here's why; the Apostle Peter told us "submit yourselves to every human authority **because of the Lord** …" Think about it; what does your submission to these human authorities have to do with the Lord? Why should Christians do this "because of" Him?

We do what God's word tells us (i.e. submit to all human authority) *because of* what Christ has done for us (i.e. "because of the Lord"). There are two related reasons why:

- **Duty:** If you're a Christian, Jesus us your King, and you owe Him your allegiance and loyalty. He speaks, and you ought to feel duty-bound to obey.
- **Love:** You're *grateful* for what He did for us, so we *want* to do what He says

Remember that, if you're a Christian, you're a priest and ambassador for God, and you need to act like one. You have a duty to represent Christ fairly and honestly to the secular authorities.[214] And, because you have love and loyalty to Christ that changes the way you live your life, you *can and must* submit yourselves to human authorities.

If that sounds hard in today's political climate in the West, then perhaps some context from Peter's era would help put things into perspective. In 62. A.D., James the Just was killed by a Jewish mob in the temple in Jerusalem, after he refused to renounce faith in Christ. This was done with the apparent blessing of the Jewish leadership, given that he was murdered in the temple. James was thrown down

---

214. On this point, see D. Edmond Hiebert, *1 Peter,* revised ed. (Winona Lake: BMH, 1992), 164-165.

from a great height from some portion of the temple, partially stoned, then had his head beaten in with a club.[215] At this time, the Roman governor Festus had recently died (see Acts 24:27f), and there was a leadership vacuum that allowed them to get away with this.

In 64 A.D., the Emperor Nero imprisoned and murdered Christians, blaming them for a massive fire which had nearly destroyed Rome.[216] You can read more contemporary tales of real persecution from publications such as *The Voice of the Martyrs,* which is available free of charge.[217]

Peter wrote this in a climate where the storm clouds of state-sanctioned persecution loomed on the horizon. The storm hadn't broken yet but, here and there, thunderclaps of local unrest signaled what would come. In that climate, Peter wrote his commands to Christians and to local churches. In the West in 2019, for most people, "persecution" means dealing with a snide comment from an unbelieving co-worker at the Keurig machine in the morning. I think we can deal with it. Peter explains (1 Pet 2:15),

> *Because this is God's will, that by doing right you'd silence the ignorant slander of foolish men.*

This is where Peter tells you *why* God wants you to do this. This is why Peter (and God!) demand you submit to all human authorities, so that you'd prove the "ignorant slander" that unbelievers spread about Christian to be wrong. What are the "good deeds" or the "doing right" that Peter is referring to?

---

215. I follow Eusebius' account, who quotes from a near-contemporary source (*Ecclesiastical History,* 2.23). Josephus makes no mention of James being clubbed to death (*Antiquities,* 20.9.1).

216. See Tacitus, "Annals 15.44.2-8," in J. Stevenson (ed.), *A New Eusebius,* revised by. W.H.C. Frend (London: SPCK, 1987), 2-3.

217. Go to https://www.persecution.com/subscribe/.

He doesn't specifically say, but they appear to be things that reflect and show God's glory to the unbelieving world; things that a priest ought to be doing to show God and His eternal Son, Jesus Christ, to unbelievers. In short, it's "doing right."

This is a blanket term, and it's hemmed in by the guardrails of 1 Peter 2:12:[218]

> *Always keep your whole way of life pure among the gentiles, so that as they speak evil about you as though you're criminals, because of your good deeds (which they're watching) they might give honor to God on that day when He returns to judge the world.*

If you're a Christian, you're God's priest, wearing His royal insignia, carrying His credentials, representing Him as an ambassador, and you're supposed to show and tell the Gospel to the world. You don't belong here, you're just a foreigner and a temporary resident. But, you can't be a priest if you wall yourselves off and live in the mountains or the desert, away from people.[219]

Peter assumes you'll be doing "good deeds" in a public and obvious way, so unbelievers will see it. He also assumes you'll be such an obvious and public part of society, that unbelievers will speak evil about you as though you're a criminal. Christians will be a thorn in a pagan world's side because we're such vocal and passionate representatives for God. When a secular society stops paying attention to Christians, then churches in that society are failing in their mission.

What's the point of all this? Why does Peter (and God!) want us to submit ourselves to those who hold power in civil office? So we'd prove the "ignorant slander of foolish men" is ridiculous and wrong.

---

218. This is my own translation.

219. See especially Karen H. Jobes, *1 Peter,* in BECNT (Grand Rapids: Baker, 2005), 176.

So we'd live the kind of life that makes people do a double-take when they compare the rhetoric with the facts of our observable life (again, see 1 Pet 2:11-12).

The point is that by living this way, as reasonable people who respect and observe the laws of the land *while* being faithful Christians, these slanderers will have no moral basis for retaliation against you (legal or otherwise); your Christian life will demonstrate you don't fit this "criminal" stereotype God's enemies are pushing!

Remember, unbelievers are speaking evil about Christians as though we're criminals, wrongdoers, deviants who don't belong in society (1 Peter 2:11-12); and the most relevant examples of this today are the areas of sexuality, abortion and religious exclusivism. In August 2017, for example, the conservative Council on Biblical Manhood and Womanhood released the Nashville Statement:[220]

This is an excellent statement that reflects traditional Christian positions on gender and sexuality. The Nashville Statement was written "in the hope of serving Christ's church and witnessing publicly to the good purposes of God for human sexuality revealed in Christian

---

220. Read the statement at https://cbmw.org/nashville-statement. The tweet can be found here: https://twitter.com/CBMWorg/status/902532283214782465.

Scripture."[221] Consider this short sample of secular and "progressive Christian" responses:[222]

---

221. From the preamble to the Nashville Statement, para. 4.

222. The interested reader can find these tweets, and many more, in response to CBMW's tweet, above. For brevity, I didn't attempt to track down every direct link for these responses.

These are not the best examples; they're just the *most appropriate* responses I can share here. But, you can see the outrage and indignation this statement has produced; it's *almost* as if they're speaking evil about Christians as though we're criminals (1 Pet 2:11-12)! In Peter's day, Christians were facing a parallel situation; they were misunderstood and marginalized by a society and culture that couldn't fathom why Christians could be such "atheists" and give honor and worship to *one God only!*

Peter is not telling you to submit to authority so you can avoid "getting in trouble" with local, state of federal government. That's not God's goal, and "getting in trouble" with the government is inevitable in a pagan culture; just ask Peter, who was martyred by the Emperor Nero not long after he wrote this letter. In the New Testament, God isn't particularly interested in your comfort in the "here and now."

This may come as a surprise to people who listen to a lot of what passes for preaching today.

Peter knows you might "get in trouble" with the government in some form or fashion, at some point in time, *because you*'re a Christian who has values and loyalties that transcend this world, and are often opposed to this world. But, Peter (and God!) want you to obey this command so that you'll honor and glorify Christ by the way you live your life. This means that, even if or when you face civil or criminal penalties for your faith, those who accuse you and those who are watching will *have to admit* they see Christ in you and they'll be forced to acknowledge that you don't fit the "criminal" stereotype they've been led to believe.

Our Western society is becoming more and more secular, and it will likely grow more and more closer to the kind of atmosphere Peter, the apostles and the early Christians ministered in. This means Christians and the state are going to come into adversarial contact more and more frequently. For example, consider a recent case involving an illegal immigrant who sought access to an abortion facility while confined at a detention facility:[223]

> Jane Doe had obtained a judge's permission to have an abortion without parental consent, as required by Texas law. A native of Central America, she entered the U.S. without a guardian and was being held in a detention center in Brownsville, Texas. She was in the official custody of the Department of Health and Human Services.
>
> "Justice prevailed today for Jane Doe," said Brigitte Amiri, senior staff attorney with the ACLU Reproductive Freedom

---

223. The following excerpt is from Bill Chappell, "'Jane Doe' Immigrant Has Abortion In Texas, After Battle With Trump Administration," from *NPR* (25OCT17). Retrieved from https://www.npr.org/sections/thetwo-way/2017/10/25/560013894/jane-doe-has-abortion-in-texas-after-battle-with-trump-administration.

Project. She added, "*With this case we have seen the astounding lengths this administration will go to block women from abortion care.*"

In court filings, Doe said that during the weeks that she was prevented from having an abortion, government agencies "forced me to obtain counseling from a religiously affiliated crisis pregnancy center where I was forced to look at the sonogram."

Shortly after this judicial ruling, the American Civil Liberties Union tweeted out this proclamation:[224]

This is but a shadow of the context Peter and the Christians he wrote to lived and ministered in – we're nowhere near that kind of pressure, but we're making some headway. Peter is saying that you're evangelizing by the way you live your life. Some of your accusers and some of those watching and cheering your persecution may not ever care about your holy way of life in the midst of this, but some will! These are the people God is reaching, and He's using your steadfastness to do it.

---

224. The tweet can be found here:
https://twitter.com/ACLU/status/923196553434673154.

- **Remember** the Philippian jailer, and Paul and Silas' example (Acts 16:16-34).
- **Remember** Pilate, and Jesus' example (see all of Luke 23; "I find no crime in this man!").
- **Remember** the thief on cross (Luke 23:39-43).

There is one classic passage that gives us some principles about how to balance God's law with man's law, and to be respectful and glorify God at the same time. That passage is Acts 5 (see also Romans 13). Paul and John had just healed a crippled man at the temple during evening prayer (see Acts 3-4). They're arrested, ordered to not preach in Jesus' name anymore, and "they let them go, finding no way to punish them, because of the people; for all men praised God for what had happened," (Acts 4:21).

Later, as they preached in the temple again, they were arrested once more. Luke's account of Peter's explanation is critical (Acts 5:27-32):

> *And when they had brought them, they set them before the council. And the high priest questioned them, saying, "We strictly charged you not to teach in this name, yet here you have filled Jerusalem with your teaching and you intend to bring this man's blood upon us."*
>
> *But Peter and the apostles answered, "We must obey God rather than men. The God of our fathers raised Jesus whom you killed by hanging him on a tree. God exalted him at his right hand as Leader and Savior, to give repentance to Israel and forgiveness of sins. And we are witnesses to these things, and so is the Holy Spirit whom God has given to those who obey him."*

What did Peter do when faced with an ultimatum? He did three things:

1. He refused, likely in a respectful way (given 1 Pet 2:13-17; cf. Acts 23:5 [cp. Exodus 22:28]).
2. He told them why ("we must obey God rather than men").
3. He explained why, and pivoted to the Gospel immediately

This passage tells us, in general terms, how we ought to implement this principle ("submit yourselves to every human authority for the Lord's sake") in everyday life:

1. Always be respectful and submissive to civil authorities.
2. If a man-made law directly contradicts God's law, politely refuse to submit, but do so in a respectful way.
3. Tell them why.
4. Explain why, and pivot to the Gospel immediately.

How Do We Do This in "Real Life?"

How do we implement these principles today, in our context? How do we submit ourselves to human authorities, while doing good and obeying God, so that we'd silence the ignorant slander of foolish men? How can you begin to do this at work, tomorrow? With your family? Friends?

Christians have always struggled to know how to apply this principle in real life, because things are often "complicated." If the Jewish leaders had said, "just don't preach or teach in Jesus' name *in the temple!*" (Acts 4:18), would Peter have refused? Or, would he have complied, and just moved operations two feet outside the temple? I don't know – this is a judgment call.

If the Jewish leaders had said, "you can preach and teach about Jesus, just not on the resurrection!," (cf. Acts 4:2) would Peter have refused? I think he would have, because it's a core doctrinal teaching.

There have been many occasions in American history where Christians have struggled to know how to balance this dilemma. The two goals are always evangelism, and faithfulness to God's word. Here are four good examples from American history which illustrate how difficult this balance can be:

The christian cake baker

If you were a Christian baker, would you bake a cake for what you *know* is a homosexual "wedding" if the laws of the State of Washington say you have to? Some Christians *wouldn't* do it – as we can tell from media coverage in recent years. Some Christians *would* do it – for equally Biblical reasons.[225]

As a way to think about this issue, consider this question - do you think the Apostle Paul only made tents for Christians? Paul was not a wealthy man, and most people in this period only earned enough to survive. Artisans made money by developing a reputation for producing better quality work than the other guy in the same town, or the next. You had to build your business locally – and this could only happen if you stayed in one place for a while, to develop a name for yourself.

Paul traveled all over for years, so it must have been extraordinarily difficult to get work – especially because the locals

---

225. The best contemporary example of the dilemma is that of Jack Phillips, a Christian cake baker. A homosexual couple sued Philips for refusing to provide a cake for a homosexual wedding, and the case eventually made its way to the U.S. Supreme Court where, as of this writing, it is awaiting a decision. For a survey of the legal case presented during oral arguments, see Tyler Robbins, "The Curious Case of the Christian Cake Baker," at *SharperIron.org* (December 11, 2017). Retrieved from https://sharperiron.org/article/curious-case-of-christian-baker-summary-of-oral-arguments.

already had their own guys they went to for tentmaking. In this context, do you actually believe Paul would have survived if he'd only made tents for Christians? I really, really, really doubt it! Can you imagine this scenario:[226]

- **Pagan:** "Hey, dude! I'd you to make me a tent."
- **Paul:** "Are you a Christian?"
- **Pagan:** "Uh . . . no, and I'm not interested. Wasn't your leader was a criminal? And, didn't he tell you guys you had to, like, eat his flesh and drink his blood, too . . . ?"."
- **Paul:** "That's not true, but I'll let it go for now. What do you plan to use the tent for?"
- **Pagan:** "I plan to use it when I make my pilgrimage to Ephesus, to worship the fertility goddess Diana. I plan to bring many cultic prostitutes back to my tent during my stay there, where we will enjoy ourselves, and I'll be praying our activities will entice the honored goddess Diana to bless me with a wife, and many sons!"
- **Paul:** "I'm sorry, pal – but I just can't allow my artistic expressions to be used for something my religion tells me is morally wrong. I suggest you try Fred, just down the road. Cheers!"

This is *my* argument, and other dedicated Christians could come up with counter-arguments (perhaps you already have!). The point is that these are tricky waters, and each Christian will have to make his own decision on where "the line" is.

---

226. You can read an extended version of this fictional dialogue at Tyler Robbins, "Paul and the Pagan – The Lost Dialogue," at *EccentricFundamentalist.com* (November 4, 2017). Retrieved from https://eccentricfundamentalist.com/2017/11/04/paul-and-the-pagan-the-lost-dialogue/.

Was the American Revolution unbiblical?

After the French-Indian War, Britain decided to begin levying a series of taxes against the American colonies. The British were in terrible debt – which happens after you fight a long and protracted war. They needed revenue; what happens when a government needs more money? It increases taxes!

The British had decided to garrison a large number of troops in America to protect settlers from encroaching on Indian lands, and to keep a wary eye on the French. Isn't is reasonable to expect the colonies to "pay their fair share" to help support troops stationed there *for their own benefit?*

However, the American colonies had no representation in Parliament at all; they had no official voice to plead their case or speak for them – this situation was the impetus for the eventual rallying cry, "no taxation without representation!" The taxes (first on sugar, then stamps, then others) caused a massive uproar in the colonies – a spark which eventually led to the American Revolution. Was this a Christian reaction?

If you're a Christian merchant and businessman in Providence, Rhode Island who imports sugar, should you try to bribe local customs officials to look the other way to not collect customs duties? Your competitors are doing it and if you pay these taxes, your business will suffer. If you were a Christian in Boston in 1770, would you join an opposition movement like "the Sons of Liberty" to subvert British rule? Is that what Jesus recommended?

When he told the Pharisees, "Render to Caesar the things that are Caesar's, and to God the things that are God's," (Mk 12:17), didn't He actually mean that? Jesus wasn't represented in the Roman Senate, was He? Was there a democratically elected Congressman from Galilee's 4th Congressional District present in Rome, representing Jesus' interests? Did the Congressman have a storefront office in downtown Nazareth? Did he hand out lawn signs for constituents to plant in their yards during election season? I doubt it.

This was a very difficult problem for Christians to deal with, and remember – we can read all about these events, but we weren't there, so we're missing something important; the passion, atmosphere and immediate context of events. I'm not advocating a position; I'm pointing out that Peter's command has real implications for real life, and Christians in America have had to deal with this before, and we will again.

Pre-Civil War era fugitive slave laws

If you were a Christian, living in America in the pre-Civil War era, would you have ignored the Federal fugitive slave laws? Article 4, Section 2 of the U.S. Constitution reads:

> *No Person held to Service or Labour in one State, under the Laws thereof, escaping into another, shall, in Consequence of any Law or Regulation therein, be discharged from such Service or Labour, but shall be delivered up on Claim of the Party to whom such Service or Labour may be due.*

This is clearly referring to African-American slaves, who were generally classified as "property" of the slaveholders in those days.[227] The Constitution doesn't say how this should be done. Eventually, a system developed where "kidnappers" (so labeled by anti-slavery advocates in the North) deployed forth in search of fugitive slaves, apprehended them, and simply brought them back South – with no legal recourse.

---

227. See the discussion of Article 4, Section 2, Clauses 2-3 from the *Constitution of the United States of America: Analysis and Interpretation* (Washington, D.C., Government Printing Office, 2016), 977-980. Retrieved from https://congress.gov/content/conan/pdf/GPO-CONAN-REV-2016-9-5.pdf.

This set up a terrible clash between pro-slavery and anti-slavery factions. The former demanded the federal government assist slaveowners in re-capturing escaped slaves who crossed state lines. The latter factions in several anti-slavery states lobbied their legislatures and successfully passed "personal liberty" laws, which gave fugitive slaves who crossed into their states certain rights (*habeas corpus*, testimony, trial by jury) and imposed criminal punishments on kidnappers.

In 1837, a man was convicted of kidnapping a former slave woman and her children from Pennsylvania, and carrying them back to Maryland (Pennsylvania had an anti-kidnapping law on its books). The U.S. Supreme Court overturned this and declared Pennsylvania's anti-kidnapping law unconstitutional and, in one stroke, invalidated similar laws in other Northern states. The Chief Justice of the U.S Supreme Court wrote that Pennsylvania's anti-kidnapping law "purports to punish as a public offence against that state, the very act of seizing and removing a slave, by his master, which the constitution of the United States was designed to justify and uphold."[228]

Nearly fourteen years later, the same Chief Justice of the Supreme Court wrote the majority decision for *Dred Scott v. Sanford*, where (among other things), he issued a decision on whether slaves could legally be considered "citizens" under the Constitution and (thus) even had the right to petition for freedom in Federal court. He declared:

> *The question before us is, whether the class of persons described in the plea in abatement compose a portion of this people, and are constituent members of this sovereignty?*
>
> *We think they are not, and that they are not included, and were not intended to be included, under the word "citizens" in*

---

228. From Chief Justice Taney's majority decision in *Prigg v. Pennsylvania* (1842). Retrieved from https://caselaw.findlaw.com/us-supreme-court/41/539.html.

> the Constitution, and can therefore claim none of the rights and privileges which that instrument provides for and secures to citizens of the United States.
>
> On the contrary, they were at that time considered as a subordinate and inferior class of beings, who had been subjugated by the dominant race, and, whether emancipated 18 or not, yet remained subject to their authority, and had no rights or privileges but such as those who held the power and the government might choose to grant them.[229]

What should devout Christians do in this environment? Pretend you're a Christian in 1856, and you live in Pennsylvania. Peter says you must submit yourselves to the civil authorities for the Lord's sake. The Federal government says it's unconstitutional to interfere with slave-owners trying to re-claim their "property" in the North. What should you do about it? How do you balance this?

In this context (and much, much more), some blacks and whites in the North decided they had to ignore Federal law and the Supreme Court in favor of what was called "higher law" doctrine (i.e. God's law). They engaged in passive resistance. They formed vigilante committees to shield and protect slaves from kidnappers, and spirit them away to Canada. This group even included clergymen from several denominations, especially in Boston. Others, like John Brown, chose the path of armed insurrection and rebellion against the Federal government

Again, I'm not advancing a position; I'm just explaining how some Christians decided to implement Peter's commands *from this passage* in real-life situations. These are tricky waters to navigate, and our waters today are just as tricky …

---

229. From Chief Justice Taney's majority decision in *Dred Scott v. Sanford* (1856). Retrieved from https://www.loc.gov/resource/llst.022.

Oregon's recent abortion law

Oregon's recent abortion law (HB 3391-B)[230] is widely acknowledged to be the most progressive and aggressive abortion law in this country. The bill requires all insurers in the State of Oregon to cover a large range of "reproductive services" (i.e. abortion) to anyone in the state – free.[231] More significantly, the bill allows a woman to get an abortion without any restriction, for any reason.[232]

---

230. See the article by Alexandra Desanctis, "Oregon Governor Puts Taxpayers on the Hook for All Abortions" in *National Review* (22AUG17). Retrieved from https://www.nationalreview.com/2017/08/oregon-abortion-law-insurance-companies-abortions/.

231. See the text of HB 3391, Section 2(3) at https://olis.leg.state.or.us/liz/2017R1/Downloads/MeasureDocument/HB3391/B-Engrossed

232. See the text of HB 3391, Section 8. It reads:

"A public body as defined in ORS 174.109 or, except as provided in ORS 435.225, an officer, employee or agent of a public body may not: (1) **Deprive a consenting individual of the choice of terminating the individual's pregnancy**; (2) Interfere with or restrict, in the regulation or provision of benefits, facilities, services or information, the choice of a consenting individual to terminate the individual's pregnancy; (3) Prohibit a health care provider, who is acting within the scope of the health care provider's license, from terminating or assisting in the termination of a patient's pregnancy; or (4) Interfere with or restrict, in the regulation or provision of benefits, facilities, services or information, the choice of a health care provider, who is acting within the scope of the health care provider's license, to terminate or assist in the termination of a patient's pregnancy."

For a legal Oregon definition of what a "public body" is, see the text of ORS 174.109 (https://www.oregonlaws.org/ors/174.109). It reads, "as used in the statutes of this state 'public body' means state government bodies, local government bodies and special government bodies."

It is clear Oregon's new legislation forbids the State from interfering with an individual's choice to terminate a pregnancy There are no exceptions listed, which is rather chilling. For example, there is no exception for late-term abortions, or sex-selective abortions. The State cannot interfere with the individual's choice. I doubt this law will go long without being challenged.

Because insurers are forbidden to pass these costs along to the consumers, the State of Oregon will be contributing about $10,000,000 to offset the proposed costs for the 2017 – 2019 biennium. This cost is expected to grow to over $14,000,000 for 2019-2021.[233] This means that, if you're an Oregon resident, your tax-dollars will be used to reimburse insurers for abortion procedures – and the costs will only go up each biennium!

What should devout Christians do in this environment? Pretend you're a Christian, and you live in Oregon. The Apostle Peter says you must submit yourselves to the civil authorities for the Lord's sake. Your believe your tax-dollars are funding the murder of unborn children. What should you do about it? How do you balance this?

Back to the Present Day

So, what should Christians do today, to put Peter's commands into practical effect in our everyday lives? Whatever course of action you take, in whatever situation you find yourself in, you have to always remember these basic principles:

1. Always be respectful
2. Always tell them why ("we must obey God rather than men," Acts 5:29)
3. Always explain why (i.e. the Gospel)

The goal is to glorify God and be a testimony for Christ; know that God wants you to submit yourself to every human authority so that, by doing right, you'd silence the ignorant slander of foolish men (1 Pet 2:15) so that they'll see your good deeds and glorify God on the day when He returns to judge the world (1 Pet 2:13).

---

233. See the State of Oregon's fiscal analysis of HB 3391 at
https://olis.leg.state.or.us/liz/2017R1/Downloads/MeasureAnalysisDocument/39461.

If those Christian men and women hadn't taken a stand for a "higher law" against the U.S. Constitution and the Supreme Court, we wouldn't know anything about it, today. You could argue their efforts were pitiful and didn't make a real difference. In terms of raw numbers, perhaps you'd be right. In terms of a testimony for God's truth about the image of God and the dignity of all men and women, you'd be wrong – because their impact couldn't be seen and weighed in their generation, you can only see its effectiveness from a distance – *which is why you can read about it today, in a history book!*

The Apostle Peter said it was God's will that, by submitting to human authorities, Christians would silence the ignorant slander of foolish men, "like freed slaves, and not like those who're wearing this freedom like a cloak of wickedness, but like God's slaves," (1 Pet 2:16).

Why does Peter say that, by doing right, we silence the ignorant slander of foolish men – like *freed* slaves; like *God's* slaves? What is he getting at? What does being a "freed slave" or "God's slave" have to do with proving ignorant slander wrong? What does it have to do with submitting to all human authority, because of the Lord?

He's referring to the *attitude* and *mindset* we should have as we "do right" and submit to secular authorities. He's referring to the *perspective* we should have of ourselves; the *view* we ought to have about who we are and what our role is *as* we go about "doing right" as secular authorities watch us during the course of our day to day lives.

Some people have a "badge" or "label" they stick themselves with, and it informs everything about them – it's the lens through which they view the world and live their lives. In the current cultural climate, your "sexual identity" or your "ethnic identity" are often the definitive markers that people use to color their entire life. And, sometimes, people sometimes identify themselves with their crippling sin (e.g. addiction, etc.). There is a better way.

If you're a Christian, your identity as "God's slave" is the marker that must dominate and inform your life, no matter what color your skin is or what evil sexual tendencies you struggle with – it's how you should "self-identify." This means we deny ourselves and do what He wants us to do, and God wants us to:

1. Submit to human authorities because of what Christ has done for you.
2. Because God's will is that, by doing right, you'd silence the ignorant slander of foolish men,
3. and He wants us to do this with the *attitude* and *mindset* that we're God's slaves, who He's freed from Satan's kingdom of darkness – so that means we can do it, even if we'd prefer to do something else

It's hard to "submit ourselves" to human authorities and respect their offices of authority, particularly when we don't personally like or respect the person holding the office, or the organization he represents! But, we do it "because of the Lord." Because he saved you. Because He transferred you out of the kingdom of darkness, and into the kingdom of His dear Son (read Col 1:13-14). Because you love Him with all your heart, soul and might (Deut 6:4). Because we consider ourselves to be dead to sin, and alive in Christ, and slaves for Him (Rom 6)

And, we submit ourselves to these authorities in a way that honors and glorifies our Lord and Savior, Jesus Christ. The Apostle Peter himself gave us the example to follow:

1. Always be respectful and submissive to civil authorities.
2. If a man-made law directly contradicts God's law, politely refuse to submit in a respectful way.
3. Tell them why.
4. Explain why, and pivot to the Gospel immediately.

Peter warns us that one way God *doesn't* want us to silence the ignorant slander of foolish men is to act like slaves who use our freedom like a cloak of wickedness. What are some ways Christians can do this?

I believe Peter is combatting the extreme idea that, because we're Christians, we have no duty to follow, obey, or submit ourselves to any authority but God. Peter is saying we have no business being political revolutionaries, arming ourselves to fight the state, or banding together to form vigilante organizations to wage guerilla war against the state.

We must *never* use our freedom from sin and adoption into Christ's family as a justification for wickedness, anarchy, rebellion against God-ordained human authorities, and the like. This kind of behavior won't silence the ignorant slander of foolish men – it'll just give them more ammunition to use against us, and it disgraces Christ and His church.

Peter finished the passage with these simple commands (1 Pet 2:17):

> *Respect all men. Love the family of believers. Always have fearful reverence for God. Always respect the Emperor.*

Together, these commands sum up what he's been telling Christians to be doing in this letter for a while now.

Respect all men

Christians, and local churches, must honor and respect everyone as human beings, made in God's image. That is not the same thing as respecting and honoring their pagan viewpoints about Biblical truth (e.g. God, Jesus, His Gospel, and all the implications of the Gospel for their lives). People's pagan viewpoints don't deserve respect, but the *people who hold them* do deserve respect – that is a critical difference.

This means we treat unbelievers with honor and respect, even when they slander us as though we're criminals; because we want them to join us on our side to glorify Christ when He returns to judge the world; because we want them to see Christ in us, and repent and believe in Him, too!

Love the family of believers

If you don't love other Christians, particularly the people in your congregation, then you're not a Christian. It's really that simple.

Always have fearful reverence for God

This attitude towards God should inform and impel everything you do and how you live your life; it's your "self-identity." You're His slave, and you live to do what He says because you love Him.

Always respect the Emperor

Again, Peter tells Christians to "always respect" the highest political authority of his day. In fact, it was the Roman Emperor Nero who was eventually responsible for Peter's death. For this principle lived out in the early post-apostolic era, see *1 Clement* 60:4 – 61:3 and *Ignatius to Ephesians* 10.

BIBLIOGRAPHY

Act of Uniformity (1559). Retrieved from the University of Hanover at https://history.hanover.edu/texts/engref/er80.html.

Act of Uniformity (1662). Retrieved from the University of London at https://www.british-history.ac.uk/statutes-realm/vol5/pp361-370/lh3 0015.

Allison, Gregg. *Sojourners and Strangers: The Doctrine of the Church,* in Foundations of Evangelical Theology, ed. John Feinberg. Wheaton: Crossway, 2012.

Alpha and Omega Ministries. "The Baptism Debate - James White vs Gregg Strawbridge." Published June 23, 2015. Retrieved from YouTube at: https://bit.ly/2Jbx8Rf.

--. "The Baptism Debate." Published March 10 2014. Retrieved from YouTube at: https://bit.ly/2GNFu39.

Armitage, Thomas. *A History of the Baptists.* New York, NY: Bryan, Taylor & Co., 1890; reprint, Watertown: Roger Williams Heritage Archive, 2003.

------------------------ "Baptist Faith and Practice," in *Baptist Doctrines,* ed. C.A. Jenkens. St. Louis: C.R. Barns, 1890; reprint; Watertown: Roger Williams Heritage Archive, 2003.

Bauder, Kevin. *Baptist Distinctives and New Testament Church Order.* Schaumberg: Regular Baptist Press, 2012.

Bauer, Walter. *A Greek-English Lexicon of the New Testament and Other Early Christian Literature*, ed. Frederick W. Danker, 3rd ed. Chicago: University of Chicago Press, 2000).

Beale, David. *Baptist History in England and America: Personalities, Positions, and Practices.* Maitland: Xulon Press, 2018.

----------------. *Historical Theology In-Depth: Themes and Contexts of Doctrinal Development Since the First Century.* Greenville: BJU Press, 2013.

Berkhof, Louis. *Systematic Theology.* Grand Rapids: Eerdmans, 1938.

Bird, Michael F. *Evangelical Theology: A Biblical and Systematic Introduction.* Grand Rapids: Zondervan, 2013.

Brackney, William H. (ed.). *Baptist Life and Thought 1600 – 1980: A Sourcebook.* Valley Forge: Judson, 1983.

Brannan, Rick (trans.). *The Apostolic Fathers in English.* Bellingham: Lexham Press, 2012.

------------------ (ed.). *The Lexham English Septuagint.* Bellingham, WA: Lexham Press, 2012.

Brown, J. Newton. "Church Covenant (1853)." Retrieved from the New Orleans Baptist Theological Seminary's *Baptist Center for Theology and Ministry* at http://www.baptistcenter.net/confessions_page.html

Busher, Leonard. "Religion's Peace, 1614," in H. Leon McBeth, *A Sourcebook for Baptist Heritage.* Nashville: Broadman, 1990.

Buswell, Jr., J. Oliver. *A Systematic Theology of the Christian Religion*, 2 vols. Grand Rapids: Zondervan, 1962.

Catechism of the Catholic Church, 2nd ed. New York: Doubleday, 1994.

Center for Reformed Theology and Apologetics. "London Baptist Confession of Faith (1689)." Retrieved from https://reformed.org/documents/index.html

----------------------------------. "Westminster Confession of Faith (1647).

----------------------------------. "Westminster Longer Catechism."

Chafer, Lewis S. *True Evangelism*. New York: Gospel Publishing House, 1911.

Chappell, Bill. "'Jane Doe' Immigrant Has Abortion In Texas, After Battle With Trump Administration." *National Public Radio* (25OCT17). Retrieved from https://www.npr.org/sections/thetwo-way/2017/10/25/560013894/jane-doe-has-abortion-in-texas-after-battle-with-trump-administration.

Christian, John T. *A History of the Baptists,* 2 vols. Texarkana: Bogard Press, 1922; Kindle reprint, 2013.

Church of England. *The 39 Articles of Religion of the Church of England (1562)*. Retrieved from https://www.churchofengland.org/prayer-and-worship/worship-texts-and-resources/book-common-prayer/articles-religion#XXVII

------------------------. *Book of Common Prayer*. Retrieved from https://www.churchofengland.org/prayer-and-worship/worship-texts-and-resources/book-common-prayer.

Clearwaters, Richard. *The Local Church of the New Testament*. Minneapolis: Central Press, 1959.

Conventicle Act (1664). Retrieved from the University of London at https://www.british-history.ac.uk/statutes-realm/vol5/pp516-520#h2-0001.

Council on Biblical Manhood and Womanhood. *Nashville Statement.* Retrieved from https://cbmw.org/nashville-statement.

Dale, R.W. *Congregational Church Polity.* London: Hodder & Stoughton, 1885.

Desanctis, Alexandra. "Oregon Governor Puts Taxpayers on the Hook for All Abortions." *National Review* (22AUG17). Retrieved from https://www.nationalreview.com/2017/08/oregon-abortion-law-insurance-companies-abortions/.

Dred Scott v. Sanford (1856). Retrieved from https://www.loc.gov/resource/llst.022.

Dyet, James. *Understanding Salvation.* Schaumberg: Regular Baptist Press, 2005.

Erickson, Millard. *Christian Theology,* 2nd ed. Grand Rapids: Baker, 1998.

Eusebius. *Ecclesiastical History,* translated by C.F. Cruse. Peabody: Hendrickson, 1998.

General Association of Regular Baptist Churches, *Articles of Faith.* Retrieved from https://www.garbc.org/about-us/beliefs-constitution/articles-of-faith/.

Guinness, Os. *The Global Public Square: Religious Freedom and the Making of a World Safe for Diversity.* Downers Grove: Zondervan, 2013.

Hammett, John. *Biblical Foundations for Baptist Churches: A Contemporary Ecclesiology.* Grand Rapids: Kregel, 2005.

Heim, Joe. "Recounting a day of rage, hate, violence and death." Washington Post, August 14, 2017.

Helwys, Thomas. "The Mistery of Iniquity," in H. Leon McBeth, *A Sourcebook for Baptist Heritage.* Nashville: Broadman, 1990.

Hiebert, D. Edmond. *1 Peter*, revised ed. Winona Lake: BMH, 1992.

Hiscox, Edward T. *Principles and Practices for Baptist Churches.* Reprint; Grand Rapids: Kregel, n.d.

Hoad, Jack. *The Baptist: An Historical and Theological Study of the Baptist Identity.* London: Grace, 1986.

Holmes, Michael. *The Apostolic Fathers*, 2nd ed. Grand Rapids: Baker, 1989.

Horton, Michael. *The Christian Faith: A Systematic Theology for Pilgrims on the Way.* Grand Rapids: Zondervan, 2011.

Hovey, Alvah. *Manual of Systematic Theology and Christian Ethics.* Boston: 1877.

Jackson, Paul R. *The Doctrine and Administration of the Church,* 3rd ed. Schaumburg: Regular Baptist Press, 2014.

Jobes, Karen H. *1 Peter*. Grand Rapids: Baker, 2005.

Josephus, Flavius. *The Works of Josephus: Complete and Unabridged.* Translated by William Whitson. Peabody: Hendrickson, 1987.

Judson, Adoniram. *Christian Baptism*. Kindle reprint; GLH Publishing, 2017.

Keach, Benjamin. *The Glory of a True Church and its Discipline display'd Wherein a true Gospel-Church is described. Together with the Power of the Keys, and who are to be let in, and who to be shut out.* London: John Robinson, 1697. Reprinted in

Mark Dever (ed.). *Polity: Biblical Arguments on How to Conduct Church Life*. Washington, D.C.: Center for Church Reform, 2001. 66-91.

Kiffin, William. *Sober Discourse of Right to Church Communion - Wherein is proved by Scripture, the example of the Primitive times, and the practice of all that Have professed the Christian Religion: That no unbaptized person may Be regularly admitted to the Lord's Supper.* London, UK. Printed by George Larkin, for Enoch Prosser, And the Rose and Crown in Sweethings - Alley, At the East End of the royal Exchange, 1681.

King, David T. *Holy Scripture: The Pillar and Ground of Our Faith*, 3 vols. Battle Ground: Christian Resources, 2001.

Kittel, Gerhard; Bromiley, Geoffrey and Friedrich, Gerhard (eds.) *Theological Dictionary of the New Testament*. Grand Rapids: Eerdmans, 1964–.

Koukl, Gregory. *The Story of Reality: How the World Began, How it Ends, and Everything Important that Happens in Between*. Grand Rapids: Zondervan, 2017.

Leeman, Jonathan. "A Congregational Approach to Unity, Holiness and Apostolicity: Faith and Order," in *Baptist Foundations: Church Government for an Anti-Institutional Age*. Nashville: B&H, 2015.

Lumpkin, William L. "The Standard Confession (1660)," in *Baptist Confessions of Faith,* revised ed. Valley Forge: Judson, 1969.

———————————— "1833 New Hampshire Confession of Faith," in *Baptist Confessions*.

———————————— "Short Confession of Faith in 20 Articles (1609)," in *Baptist Confessions*.

---------------------------- "London Confession" (1644), in *Baptist Confessions.*

---------------------------- "Somerset Confession" (1656)," in *Baptist Confessions.*

---------------------------- "A Short Confession" 1610," in *Baptist Confessions.*

McBeth, H. Leon. *The Baptist Heritage.* Nashville: B&H, 1987.

McCune, Rolland. *A Systematic Theology of Biblical Christianity*, 3 vols. Detroit: DBTS, 2010.

Merkle, Benjamin. "The Scriptural Basis for Elders," in *Baptist Foundations: Church Government for an Anti-Institutional Age.* Nashville: B&H, 2015.

Merriam-Webster Collegiate Dictionary, 11th ed. Springfield: Merriam-Webster, 2003.

Moo, Douglas J. *The Epistle to the Romans.* Grand Rapids: Eerdmans, 1996.

Murray, John. *The Epistle to the Romans*, combined ed. Grand Rapids: Eerdmans, 1968.

Mullins, E.Y. *The Axioms of Religion.* Philadelphia: American Baptist Publication Society, 1908; reprint; Watertown, WI: Roger Williams Heritage Archives, 2003.

Oats, Larry. "GPA 614 - Baptist Policy," Summer 2013, unpublished class notes. Watertown: Maranatha Baptist Seminary.

Oregon HB 3391. Retrieved from https://olis.leg.state.or.us/liz/2017R1/Downloads/MeasureDocument/HB3391/B-Engrossed

Prigg v. Pennsylvania (1842). Retrieved from https://caselaw.findlaw.com/us-supreme-court/41/539.html

Reymond, Robert. *A New Systematic Theology of the Christian Faith*, 2nd ed. Nashville: Thomas Nelson, 1998.

Robbins, Tyler. "What is 'Landmarkism?' A Quick Look at a Strange Baptist Polity." *Eccentric Fundamentalist*, published on August 6, 2014 at https://bit.ly/2IAn5rA.

------------------. "The Curious Case of the Christian Cake Baker." SharperIron.org, published on December 11, 2017. Retrieved from https://sharperiron.org/article/curious-case-of-christian-baker-summary-of-oral-arguments

------------------. "Paul and the Pagan – The Lost Dialogue." *Eccentric Fundamentalist*, published on November 4, 2017. Retrieved from https://eccentricfundamentalist.com/2017/11/04/paul-and-the-pagan-the-lost-dialogue/.

Schaff, Phillip (ed.). "The Council of Trent, Seventh Session, Canon 4," in *The Creeds of Christendom*, 3 vols. New York: Harper & Brothers, 1890.

--------------------------. "Luther's Small Catechism," Part 5, in *The Creeds of Christendom*, 3 vols. New York: Harper & Brothers, 1890.

--------------------------. "The Augsburg Confession," Second Part, in *The Creeds of Christendom*, 3 vols. New York: Harper & Brothers, 1890.

--------------------------. *History of the Christian Church*, 8 vols. New York: Charles Scribner's Sons, 1910.

--------------------------. "The Belgic Confession," Article 29, in *The Creeds of Christendom*, 3 vols. New York: Harper & Brothers, 1882.

Schreiner, Thomas. "Baptism in the Bible," in *Baptist Foundations: Church Government for an Anti-Institutional Age.* Nashville: B&H, 2015.

Silva, Moises. *New International Dictionary of New Testament Theology and Exegesis.* 5 vols. Grand Rapids: Zondervan, 2014.

Smyth, John. "On Religious Liberty," from H. Leon McBeth, *A Sourcebook for Baptist Heritage.* Nashville: B&H, 1990.

Strong, Augustus H. *Systematic Theology.* Old Tappan: Fleming H. Revell, 1907.

Southern Baptist Convention, *2000 Baptist Faith and Message.* Retrieved from http://www.sbc.net/bfm2000/bfm2000.asp.

Tacitus. "Annals 15.44.2-8," in J. Stevenson (ed.), *A New Eusebius*, revised by. W.H.C. Frend. London: SPCK, 1987.

Tanner, Norman J. (ed.). *Decrees of the Ecumenical Councils.* 2 vols. Washington D.C., Georgetown University Press, 1990.

Tappert, Theodore G. (ed.). "Luther's Large Catechism," in *The Book of Concord.* Philadelphia: Fortress, 1959.

------------------------------------. "Apology of the Augsburg Confession," Article 15, in *The Book of Concord*.

------------------------------------. "Augsburg Confession," Article 27, in *The Book of Concord.*

Theissen, Henry. *Introductory Lectures in Systematic Theology.* Grand Rapids: Eerdmans, 1949.

U.S. Government Printing Office. *Constitution of the United States of America: Analysis and Interpretation.* Washington, D.C., Government Printing Office, 2016. Retrieved from https://congress.gov/content/conan/pdf/GPO-CONAN-REV-2016-9-5.pdf.

Vogel, Jim (ed.). *The Pastor: A Guide for God's Faithful Servant* Schaumberg: Regular Baptist Press, 2012.

Waldron, Samuel and Richard Barcellos. *A Reformed Baptist Manifesto: The New Covenant Constitution of the Church*. Palmdale: RBAP, 2004.

Weston, Henry G. "Baptism – A Symbol," in *The Madison Avenue Lectures*. Reprint; Watertown: Roger Williams Heritage Archives, 2003.

Scripture Index

Genesis

Gen 3:15 .... 29, 49
Gen 12:3 29

Exodus

Ex 19:5-6 162
Ex 22:28 204
Ex 24:1-8 88

Leviticus

Lev 1:1-5 158
Lev 1:5 85
Lev 5:9 85
Lev 5:16 85
Lev 13 158
Lev 16:30 158

Deuteronomy

Deut 6:4 214
Deut 6:4-5 23
Deut 6:5 45
Deut 6:20-25 45
Deut 10:16 .... 53, 71
Deut 18:15-19 29

2 Kings

2 Kgs 5:10 (LXX) 77
2 Kgs 5:14 .... 77, 82

1 Chronicles

1 Chr 17:11-15 29

2 Chronicles

2 Chr 3:10-14 159

Ezra

Ezra 8:1-9 158

Psalms

Ps 2 29
Ps 16 31
Ps 51:2 83
Ps 51:7 83
Ps 110:1 30
Ps 110:4 30
Ps 119:105 35

Proverbs

Prov 30:12 83

Isaiah

Isa 1:16 84
Isa 1:17 84
Isa 11:2 30
Isa 21:4 .... 78, 82
Isa 28:17-18 161
Isa 32:15 84
Isa 42:6 49

Reference	Page
Isa 44:3	85
Isa 52:15	85
Isa 56	59

Jeremiah

Reference	Page
Jer 2:22	84
Jer 4:4	53
Jer 4:14	84
Jer 31	44
Jer 31:31-34	39, 112

Ezekiel

Reference	Page
Ezek 11:17-20	39
Ezek 16:59-63	40
Ezek 36:22-32	112
Ezek 36:24-31	41
Ezek 36:25	67, 85, 90
Ezek 36:26-27	49
Ezek 39:29	85

Daniel

Reference	Page
Dan 4:3 (LXX)	124
Dan 6 (LXX)	124

Joel

Reference	Page
Joel 2:28	85

Zechariah

Reference	Page
Zech 3	30
Zech 3:8	30
Zech 9:9	42
Zech 9:11-12	42

Matthew

Mt 1:1	29
Mt 3:11	86
Mt 3:16	79
Mt 3:8	185
Mt 4:19	28
Mt 10:2	136
Mt 26:26	97
Mt 26:28	98
Mt 28:19	109
Mt 28:19-20	11, 32

Mark

Mk 1:8	42, 62, 67, 76, 86, 112
Mk 1:10	76
Mk 1:14-15	30
Mk 1:15	174
Mk 2:17	174
Mk 3:14	136
Mk 3:21	80
Mk 6:12	174
Mk 6:30	136
Mk 7:3-4	80, 82
Mk 12:17	207
Mk 12:29-31	23
Mk 14:22	97, 102
Mk 14:24	98
Mk 14:61-64	31
Mk 15:31-32	174
Mk 15:37-38	159
Mk 16:15-16	49

Luke

Lk 2:1	124
Lk 4:18-19	30
Lk 6:13	136
Lk 7:18-23	30
Lk 9:10	136
Lk 11:20-22	31

Lk 11:38	80
Lk 11:49	136
Lk 17:5	136
Lk 20:19	98
Lk 20:19-26	189
Lk 20:20	98
Lk 22:14	136
Lk 22:19	97, 104
Lk 22:20	49, 97
Lk 22:35-38	189
Lk 22:47-51	189
Lk 23	203
Lk 23:2	189
Lk 23:39-43	203
Lk 24:10	136
Lk 24:49	25, 86

John

Jn 1:26-27	86
Jn 3:5	42, 86
Jn 3:16	49
Jn 3:23	81, 82
Jn 5:26	159
Jn 6:44-45	49
Jn 13:10	87
Jn 13:16	136
Jn 14:15-17	26
Jn 14:16	25
Jn 14:23	25
Jn 14:26	15, 25
Jn 14:30-31	31

Acts

Acts 1:4	25
Acts 1:5	86
Acts 1:6-11	32
Acts 1:8	27, 86, 136
Acts 2	36

Acts 2:1-7	25
Acts 2:4	86
Acts 2:4, 13	175
Acts 2:22-36	73
Acts 2:23-24	31
Acts 2:25-33	31
Acts 2:33	25, 71, 86
Acts 2:37	136
Acts 2:37-41	56
Acts 2:38	25
Acts 2:42	136
Acts 2:43	136
Acts 3-4	203
Acts 4	195
Acts 4:2	205
Acts 4:8	25
Acts 4:18	204
Acts 4:21	203
Acts 4:31	25
Acts 4:33	136
Acts 4:35, 37	136
Acts 5	203
Acts 5:1-11	136
Acts 5:2	136
Acts 5:12	136
Acts 5:17, 27-32	136
Acts 5:17-18	136
Acts 5:19-20	136
Acts 5:27-32	203
Acts 5:29	212
Acts 5:30-32	25
Acts 6:1-6	136, 149
Acts 6:1-6	150
Acts 6:3	25, 150
Acts 7:55-56	25
Acts 8:1	119, 137
Acts 8:3	119
Acts 8:4	119
Acts 8:5-8	119
Acts 8:12-13	57

Reference	Page
Acts 8:14-16	137
Acts 8:14-17	25, 119
Acts 8:16	86
Acts 8:25	119
Acts 8:26-38	119
Acts 8:34-38	58
Acts 8:36-39	81, 82
Acts 8:39	119
Acts 8:40	119
Acts 9:1-9	119
Acts 9:10	119
Acts 9:14-19	25
Acts 9:19	119
Acts 9:23-25	120
Acts 9:25	119
Acts 9:27	137
Acts 9:31	120
Acts 10:22-24	25
Acts 10:34-43	59
Acts 10:44	86
Acts 10:44-46	25
Acts 10:44-48	58
Acts 10:46	86
Acts 10:47	59
Acts 11:15	86
Acts 11:15-18	25
Acts 11:19	120
Acts 11:23	120
Acts 11:25-26	120
Acts 11:26	121
Acts 11:29-30	120
Acts 11:30	139, 147
Acts 12:1-3	189
Acts 12:5	189
Acts 13:2-3	120
Acts 13:9	25
Acts 13:52	25
Acts 14:4, 14	137
Acts 14:23	147
Acts 14:26-28	120

Acts 15	118, 121, 127
Acts 15:2	137
Acts 15:2, 4, 6	147
Acts 15:4ff	137
Acts 15:8	25
Acts 15:22-23	147
Acts 15:28	25
Acts 15:36	123
Acts 15:41	123
Acts 16:1-2	126
Acts 16:4	123, 137, 147
Acts 16:5	126
Acts 16:11-15	126
Acts 16:14-15	59
Acts 16:16-34	203
Acts 16:19-24	189
Acts 16:29-34	60
Acts 16:31	61
Acts 16:32	61
Acts 16:34	61
Acts 16:35-40	190
Acts 16:40	126
Acts 17:1-9	126
Acts 17:7	124
Acts 17:10	126
Acts 17:14	126
Acts 17:34	126
Acts 18:1-11	126
Acts 18:8	61
Acts 18:22	126
Acts 18:23	126
Acts 19:1-7	25, 62
Acts 19:2	62
Acts 19:10	126
Acts 19:22	126
Acts 19:23-41	126
Acts 20:1	126
Acts 20:17	127, 148
Acts 20:20	139
Acts 20:27-30	139

Acts 20:28	148
Acts 20:28-29	139
Acts 21:7	127
Acts 21:16	127
Acts 21:18	147
Acts 21:20-25	122
Acts 22:16	63, 86
Acts 23:1-5	190
Acts 23:5	204
Acts 24:27	196

Romans

Rom 1:1	137
Rom 1:18-23	23
Rom 3:20-21	49
Rom 5:18-19	64
Rom 5:20	64
Rom 6	91
Rom 6:1	64
Rom 6:1-11	63
Rom 6:2	64
Rom 6:3	64
Rom 6:4	64
Rom 6:5	64, 65
Rom 6:6	64
Rom 6:7	64
Rom 6:8	64
Rom 6:9	64
Rom 6:10	64, 65
Rom 6:11	65
Rom 6:12	65
Rom 6:13	65
Rom 6:14	65
Rom 6:22	65
Rom 8:3	49
Rom 8:8	23
Rom 8:9-11	24
Rom 10:6, 9	49
Rom 11:13	137

Rom 13 203
Rom 16:7 137

1 Corinthians

1 Cor 1:1 .... 66, 137
1 Cor 1:2 10
1 Cor 1:13-16 66
1 Cor 3:5-7 29
1 Cor 3:10-15 143
1 Cor 3:11-15 174
1 Cor 5 128
1 Cor 5:1 184
1 Cor 5:5 186
1 Cor 5:6-7 186
1 Cor 5:9-11 186
1 Cor 5:12-13 187
1 Cor 6:9-11 67
1 Cor 6:11 87
1 Cor 9:1 137
1 Cor 9:5 137
1 Cor 9:24-27 82
1 Cor 10:2 .... 81, 82
1 Cor 10:6 82
1 Cor 11:23-24 99
1 Cor 11:25 .... 49, 99, 104
1 Cor 11:26 .... 35, 99, 104
1 Cor 12:7 67
1 Cor 12:12-13 67
1 Cor 12:13 27
1 Cor 12:14 68
1 Cor 12:28 137
1 Cor 15:3-7 31
1 Cor 15:7 138
1 Cor 15:9 137

2 Corinthians

2 Cor 1:1 .... 10, 137
2 Cor 8-9 129

2 Cor 11:5, 13... 138
2 Cor 12:11 138
2 Cor 12:12 138

Galatians

Gal 1:1... 137
Gal 1:2... 10
Gal 1:4... 73
Gal 2:21... 144
Gal 3:11... 49
Gal 3:21... 49
Gal 3:23-27 68
Gal 5:16-26 26

Ephesians

Eph 1:1.. 69, 137
Eph 1:12.. 23
Eph 2:10.. 19
Eph 2:15.. 124
Eph 2:20.. 138
Eph 3:5.. 138
Eph 4:1-5... 71
Eph 4:1-6... 69
Eph 4:4-6... 16
Eph 4:11.. 139
Eph 5:26.. 87

Philippians

Phil 1:1 .... 10, 139, 148
Phil 2 31

Colossians

Col 1:1... 137
Col 1:13-14 214
Col 1:2.. 10
Col 2:8-15... 69

Col 2:14 125
Col 3:16-17 24

1 Thessalonians

1 Thess 1:1 10
1 Thess 1:2-3 28
1 Thess 1:5 28
1 Thess 1:6 28
1 Thess 1:8 28
1 Thess 1:9 28
1 Thess 1:10 28
1 Thess 2:6 137
1 Thess 4:16-17 9
1 Thess 5:12 148
1 Thess 5:13 148

2 Thessalonians

2 Thess 1:1 10

1 Timothy

1 Tim 1:1 137
1 Tim 2:7 137
1 Tim 3:1 148
1 Tim 3:2 139
1 Tim 3:8-13 149
1 Tim 5:17 .... 139, 148

2 Timothy

2 Tim 1:1 137
2 Tim 1:3-7 146
2 Tim 1:11 137
2 Tim 1:13 .... 32, 146
2 Tim 1:14 147
2 Tim 2:1-2 147
2 Tim 2:3-10 147
2 Tim 2:5 163

2 Tim 2:11-14 ... 147
2 Tim 2:14-18 ... 147
2 Tim 2:15 ... 143
2 Tim 2:22-23 ... 147
2 Tim 2:24-26 ... 147

Titus

Titus 1:1 ... 137
Titus 1:5 ... 148
Titus 1:7 ... 139, 148
Titus 2:11-14 ... 35
Titus 3:3-7 ... 71, 76
Titus 3:4-7 ... 87
Titus 3:5 ... 87

Hebrews

Heb 1:3 ... 88
Heb 2:10 ... 159
Heb 2:14-15 ... 31, 65
Heb 4:14-16 ... 159
Heb 7 ... 30
Heb 7:22 ... 49
Heb 7:23-25 ... 163
Heb 7:25 ... 164
Heb 7:26-28 ... 30
Heb 8 ... 43
Heb 8:6 ... 30
Heb 8:6-18 ... 97
Heb 9:7 ... 43
Heb 9:9 ... 43
Heb 9:14 ... 88
Heb 9:15-17 ... 49
Heb 9:22 ... 88
Heb 9:23-26 ... 88
Heb 9:26-28 ... 97
Heb 10:2 ... 88
Heb 10:4 ... 89
Heb 10:10 ... 89

Heb 10:11-22	43
Heb 10:12-18	98
Heb 10:19-22	72
Heb 10:22	89
Heb 13:7	148
Heb 13:12	89
Heb 13:17	148
Heb 13:20	89

James

Jas 1:1	10
Jas 4:8	89
Jas 5:14	148

1 Peter

1 Pet 1:1	10, 137
1 Pet 1:2	89
1 Pet 1:17	174
1 Pet 1:22	27
1 Pet 2:4-10	19, 160
1 Pet 2:6	161
1 Pet 2:6-8	161
1 Pet 2:8-10	162
1 Pet 2:9-10	14
1 Pet 2:11-12	198, 200
1 Pet 2:12	197
1 Pet 2:13	212
1 Pet 2:13-17	188, 204
1 Pet 2:15	196, 212
1 Pet 2:16	213
1 Pet 2:17	215
1 Pet 2:25	139
1 Pet 3:18	97
1 Pet 3:19-22	72
1 Pet 3:20-21	89
1 Pet 3:21	76
1 Pet 4:1-3	19
1 Pet 4:7-11	20

1 Pet 4:11	142
1 Pet 5:1	148
1 Pet 5:1-10	148
1 Pet 5:1-2	140, 141
1 Pet 5:2, 4	139
1 Pet 5:2-5	145
1 Pet 5:5	148

2 Peter

2 Pet 1:1	137
2 Pet 1:3	15
2 Pet 3:2	138

2 John

2 Jn 1:1	148

3 John

3 Jn 1:1	148

Jude

Jude 17	138

Revelation

Rev 1-3	10
Rev 2:2	138
Rev 20:11-15	174
Rev 21:14	138

Magnesians

Mag 13:1	125

Barnabas

Bar 1:6	125

1 Clement

1 Clem 129
1 Clem 60:4 - 61:3 216

Didache

Did 11:3 125

Ignatius to the Ephesians

Ignatius to Eph 10 216

Judith

Judith 12:7 .... 78, 82

Made in the USA
Coppell, TX
11 November 2020